BOTH SIDES OF THE COIN
THE ARGUMENTS AGAINST THE EURO

The euro was introduced in Euroland on 1 January 1999 and goes into everyday use on 1 January 2002. Will it usher in a new era of prosperity for Europe or will it precipitate financial disaster? What will be its effect on jobs? And on interest rates and mortgages?

The single currency fills the pages of the newspapers every day, but the arguments against the euro are never set out clearly and concisely. Here, in an elegant essay by one of Britain's leading economists, are the powerful arguments for remaining outside the single currency. James Forder lucidly explains the arguments against the euro – deflationary pressure, high risk of failure, small upside and its anti-democratic management – and he shows why the advantages have been overstated.

James Forder makes the case against joining the euro persuasively and convincingly.

For the arguments for, turn this book over.

BOTH SIDES OF THE COIN

THE ARGUMENTS AGAINST THE EURO

by

James Forder

P

PROFILE BOOKS

First published in Great Britain in 1999 by
Profile Books Ltd
58A Hatton Garden
London EC1N 9LX
www.profilebooks.co.uk

This second edition published in 2001

1 3 5 7 9 10 8 6 4 2

Typeset in Galliard by MacGuru
info@macguru.org.uk
Printed and bound in Great Britain by
Bookmarque Ltd, Croydon, Surrey

A CIP catalogue record for this book is available from the British Library.

ISBN 1 86197 321 7

Contents

The author

James Forder is a Fellow of Balliol College, Oxford, where he teaches economics. He was senior tutor of the Oxford University Business Economics Programme and has also taught aspects of the politics and economics of European integration at La Sorbonne, at Chulalongkorn University, Bangkok, and in Japan. His previous publications include *The European Union and National Macroeconomic Policy*, edited with Anand Menon, which considered the evolution of economic policy-making in the European Union, and other essays on European economics and central bank independence. He always thought of himself as a Euroenthusiast until the Maastricht Treaty came to dominate European politics and made that position impossible for a liberal economist.

Preface and acknowledgements

This second edition is really another book, as we now have facts not just hypotheses. Eleven countries adopted the euro on 1 January 1999, and a twelfth – Greece – joined the euro group on 1 January 2001. So the euro has begun. All twelve countries will replace their national notes and coin with the new euro in the first part of 2002, and British holidaymakers will start to use euros for the first time that summer.

The debate about British membership will not go away. It is one of those defining issues which can reshape old loyalties. In this context, there has been a lot of low political debate that has largely used whatever projectiles happened to be at hand. But there has been too little elucidation of the real economic and political issues, although there could hardly be something more economic and political than the decision to adopt a new currency. We aim to fill the gap.

We have embarked upon the book in this form – in two halves, with a case for and a case against – to highlight the issues behind the decision. Although this is an argument, it is also designed to ensure that any intelligent reader of a British newspaper is able to cut through the chaff in the debate and focus on the important points. We have, however, imposed certain rules on ourselves. The data cited on each side in this book are not in dispute between us. What clearly differentiates us are matters of interpretation. How much weight should be given to one factor or another?

Every book of this kind owes a great debt to the others that have gone before. Thanks are also due to colleagues who directly or indirectly helped to shape some of these arguments. Chris Huhne particularly thanks Michael Emerson, with whom he wrote a previous book on the single currency dealing with the general arguments applicable to Europe as a whole, Lillian Andenaes, whose research assistance in this second edition has been vital, and Sebastien Clerc-Renaud for statistical support. Chris would also like to thank specifically John Arrowsmith, Nick Clegg, Andrew Duff, Will Hutton, Richard Portes, Lionel Price, Vicky Pryce, Kitty Ussher and William Wallace for reading part or all of the manuscript in one or two editions and for helping to excise several errors of fact and interpretation. James Forder particularly thanks John Arrowsmith, Donna Bellingham, Ann Branch, Dominic Cumings, Andrew Haldenby, Allison Hoffman, Anand Menon, Malcolm Walter and Peter Oppenheimer. Those errors that remain are, of course, ours.

James Forder and Christopher Huhne
May 2001

1 Introduction and summary

Euroscepticism is no longer the preserve of nationalists, eccentrics and little-Englanders but has become a cause for the liberal conscience. The Maastricht Treaty has created a monetary union which poses great threats to the prosperity, unity and internationalism of the European Union and to the stability of its member states. The Treaty is based on bad economics and on the foolish view that a common money will promote harmony, irrespective of its management and regardless of its economic consequences.

It is a tragedy that the European Union has adopted this plan, but we cannot help it and probably never could have. There is nothing for us to do now except avoid embroiling ourselves in Europe's mistake. Britain will then be standing aside, not because of a hallucination of national superiority, or a fatal desire for independence in an interdependent world, or an inflated vision of the importance of our history, language, legal system or culture. We shall be standing aside because political ideology should not overrule economic sense; because of a concern that a balance of economic objectives be pursued, not just those of certain interests; and because of a sense of the vulnerability of liberal, democratic and internationalist institutions – European and national – to economic failure.

None of this means that one should doubt that the goal of economic and monetary union (EMU) began as the best of European objectives. It was a dream, perhaps a fantasy, but the aim was for unity, internationalism, prosperity and justice. All these were to be promoted, not just symbolised, by the common currency. The first attempt, known as the Werner Plan, made an unfortunate and unachievable commitment to monetary union by 1980. The fear of another failure like that still distorts thinking on the issue. The next attempt to move towards monetary co-operation, the European Monetary System (EMS), began operating in 1979. It functioned well for several years, reducing the short-term volatility of both exchange rates and interest rates, without any particular need for a common currency being perceived.[1]

By the end of the 1980s European prospects seemed excellent. The growth of the European economies seemed likely to speed up and unemployment to fall after a protracted period of inflation-fighting earlier in the decade. There was a new consensus on the right way to conduct economic policy, based on low inflation and sound finance, which many people expected to bring sustained prosperity. The collapse of communist regimes was widely expected to create a great investment opportunity and itself to be likely to further economic growth and political integration in Europe. There also appeared to be a new prospect of faster and deeper European integration. Rapid progress was being made towards the implementation of the 1992 single market project; Britain joined the EMS; and slightly later, after a change of prime minister, the British government even professed itself seeking to be 'at the heart of Europe'. It was in this environment that a new plan for monetary union, the Maastricht plan, based on central bank independence, price stability and low government borrowing, was agreed, with initially only Britain refraining from a full commitment to joining by 1999 at the latest.

Since then things have been more difficult. A rapid acceleration of growth did not materialise. Indeed, unemployment rates began to rise again from already high levels. East European reform was not the immediate success that had been hoped. Inflation remained low, but government finances deteriorated markedly, creating doubt in many minds as to whether the monetary union plan should be implemented. One reason was that it had been made a condition of participation that countries have low enough government borrowing – less than 3 per cent of national output – and a low enough volume of debt outstanding – less than 60 per cent of national output.[2] As the 1990s progressed many countries seemed likely to miss these targets. Eventually, it was decided that all countries except Greece were 'moving in the right direction', and by virtue of this, rather than of having arrived, were qualified to join. By this time Denmark had decided against joining, and of three new members of the European Union (Sweden, Finland and Austria) Sweden also chose to wait. Thus eleven countries remained eligible and committed when it was finally decided to proceed.

Much of the distress of the European economies in this period is attributable to German unification, German monetary union and the policies which followed. Nevertheless, events have demonstrated the deficiencies of the Maastricht plan. Unification took place before Maastricht, but it had been expected to create great investment opportunities and therefore to be on the whole economically beneficial. The outcome was rather different. The Bundesbank chose to regard a small rise in prices as a major threat to economic stability and began raising interest rates. This contributed to what became a long and deep recession in Germany, accompanied by spiralling government debt and the highest unemployment rate Germany had experienced since the Great Depression. German monetary union is not really a good test of the desirability of EMU since a number of the circumstances are different. But the outcome is certainly not a good omen either.

Most of the other EU member states felt forced to raise their interest rates as well, although they were, on the basis of their own economies, in need of lower rates not higher ones. The reason they did this is that higher interest rates in Germany make Deutschmark assets more attractive to investors, leading to the purchase of Deutschmarks and the sale of other currencies.[3] If this had been allowed to occur on a sufficient scale it would have forced the devaluation of the other currencies or, equivalently, the upward valuation of the Deutschmark. The French, in particular, were unwilling to devalue the franc and preferred therefore to see France as well as Germany fall deeper and deeper into recession. This is the origin of the great, prolonged European recession of the 1990s. It lies in the policy response to German unification in Germany and in the rest of continental Europe. It is no easy matter to pin down just why this policy was followed, but three different stories are told.

The first is simply that the Maastricht Treaty and associated 'gentlemen's agreements' obliged the countries concerned to keep their exchange rates fixed. If so, it is a good demonstration of how easy it is for the European Union to get itself into a position where a serious economic problem arises that the political process cannot readily fix; how political momentum can dominate good economics; and how dangerous it is to suppose that things will inevitably be worked out for the best when commitments have been made to the contrary. All those who see deficiencies in the plan for monetary union, but suppose that they will all be solved if Britain joins should take heed of the lessons of history.

The second story is that French policymakers believed that any devaluation of the franc would inevitably lead to inflation in France, and the rest of continental Europe took France's lead. This argument is not correct since the change in the French price level depends on the level of unemployment in France as well as the exchange rate. Devaluations in recessions, when accompanied by appropriate policies, have been extremely effective in restoring prosperity without raising inflation to any significant extent. Britain in 1992 is an obvious example. There are also examples of failed devaluations, such as the French ones of 1981 and 1983. But they failed, leading to inflation, because the rest of the French policy was inflationary when the opposite was required. The claim that devaluations are never effective is either derived from a very limited theory, or it is false.

The third story is that French policymakers feared for their credibility. That is, it was not the devaluation itself that was thought undesirable, but rather the demonstration of a willingness to devalue. Currency markets, so the argument runs, would forever expect that further devaluations were imminent and the franc would be bedevilled by permanent speculation. This argument has also been shown to be nonsense by the British experience since 1992. An initial devaluation was not met by continuing speculation on further falls. Indeed, it was not long before a rising, not a falling, pound became evident. Nevertheless, the doctrine of credibility continues to have a powerful influence on European thinking. The suspicion that this was at least part of the reason the French chose damaging interest-rate increases rather than an appropriate devaluation should also be a warning that concern with 'credibility' can appear to justify all kinds of foolish policy.

Meanwhile, Britain, having joined the exchange-rate mechanism of the EMS in 1990 after years of dispute within the government, also found itself with an overvalued currency. Many jobs were lost and much money spent in the attempt to maintain the rate. Ultimately, it proved impossible and devaluation and a much-improved economy followed. It is a pity that devaluation did not come earlier, but at least it came, in contrast to France.

These developments should in themselves demonstrate the folly of EMU. A policy was adopted in Germany that was quite simply inappropriate for France, Britain, Italy and the rest of the EMS. This is the key cost of a single currency: that every member country must have the same interest rate regardless of its circumstances. No one need look further for an example of the damage EMU can do: the developments following German unification are a perfect case.

In Britain advocates of the euro argue that our EMS experience shows nothing because we joined at the wrong time, when the pound was overvalued. This may be true, but there are few advocates of British membership of the euro now who were not advocates of the EMS in 1990, and at that time they had as little patience with the view that the time was not right as they do today with the same argument about the euro. In any case, this view offers no kind of answer to the question of what caused the great European recession. The other countries had been in the EMS for years.

In France, however, a more important mistake has been made. This is to suppose that the problems of the French economy would have been avoided if there had been joint control over monetary policy in the EMS, rather than everyone in practice following the lead of the Bundesbank. From this perspective EMU solves the problem, since it means there will be international control over policy.

But this is no solution at all from the point of view of Europe as a whole. Certainly, the problem faced by the French was that they found themselves in the position where the Germans were setting policy. But, on the assumption that this policy was the best for Germany, having someone else set policy, such as an international committee of bankers as the Maastricht Treaty does, can make policy better for France only by making it worse for Germany. Fundamentally, what the case of German unification demonstrates is not the cost of having German policy applied throughout Europe, but the cost of having any single policy applied.

It can be said, in defence of EMU, that German unification was a one-off event, never to be repeated, but it is a frail defence. It is in the nature of events dangerous to the euro area that they are unpredictable. Unification is merely an example of the kind of problem that can arise, and when it does arise is serious. Different circumstances in different countries lead to a desire for different policies, but a monetary union forces us all to have the same policy.

A further lesson can be drawn from the experience of the whole of Europe, including Britain, since the early 1980s. Around that time it became fashionable in economic policymaking circles to suppose that inflation is the only true economic evil. If only price stability could be achieved, it was supposed, everything else would fall into place. Unemployment would look after itself, and the forces of the market would deliver rapid economic growth and prosperity. Certainly, an emphasis on the control of inflation was appropriate in many countries for much of the 1980s, but it is now clear that the wider promise has not been fulfilled.

THE ARGUMENTS AGAINST THE EURO

The crucial point is that unemployment does not 'look after itself' and return to a low level once inflation has been eliminated. Long and deep recessions can result in unemployment remaining high for many years after inflation has been eliminated. This means that policymakers cannot afford to think only in terms of the control of inflation. They must recognise other objectives as quite proper as well.

Unfortunately, in 1991 the Maastricht Treaty was written to codify the policy presumptions of that time in the future monetary union. Consequently, the European Central Bank (ECB) is obliged to pursue price stability, whatever the cost in unemployment and growth. It is to be left entirely free of any kind of control in doing this. To make matters worse, the use of fiscal policy (that is, the balance of government taxation and expenditure) is also to be severely restricted so that a potentially important mitigating force will probably be devoid of significant power.

The advocates of EMU are in two minds about how to respond to this point. On one hand, people such as Emerson and others, who were writing on behalf of the European Commission,[4] take the line that the control of inflation is indeed the only proper objective of policy. In this case the unaccountability of the ECB and its exclusive focus on inflation are benefits of the euro. On the other hand, as I shall argue in Chapter 3, these views are hard to sustain when looking at the actual course of unemployment in Europe. Consequently, others among the advocates of the euro are inclined to say that no one could possibly take the Treaty literally and that the ECB will take a far more balanced view than it suggests and be far more responsive to the European democracies. The difficulty for this group, of course, is what to say about the first group. Many advocates of integration evidently do believe that the Treaty should be followed to the letter, and this appears to be true of the staff of the ECB itself.

Furthermore, the Treaty plays into the hands of those who would have this policy followed by giving it legal backing. This point i̇s illuṡtrated by the behaviour of the Monetary Policy Committee (

the Bank of England. Many people have called for lower interest rates and accused the MPC of being insufficiently representative of the regions or industry, or of knowing too little about the real world. Members of the MPC have made many speeches, answering that this is an unfair charge because they are simply doing as they are told: trying to achieve a specific inflation outcome as set by the government. There is no reason to think that individuals more representative of industry would be better able to achieve this outcome and therefore, they argue, there is no case to answer. They are right, of course, as far as they go. But the appropriate question is whether they should have been given this task in the first place; whether it might not have been better to recognise that this policy would have undesirable side effects, such as an excessive rise in the value of the pound, which has risked permanent damage to British exports.

The members of the MPC have not had to address the question of whether their policy is good policy, and have stuck to the claim that it is the policy they have been told to follow. Why would we expect the ECB, which will certainly be much more firmly under the sway of anti-inflationary interests, to take a different view? The ECB will argue that it is legally required to pursue price stability above all other goals, and therefore complaints about its failure to recognise other goals are beside the point.

In the British case the government has specifically retained authority to change the instructions given to the Bank of England, and it is reasonable to entertain the hope that this will be done if the need is sufficiently clear. In the European case such a change would necessitate a Treaty amendment which is a lengthy process requiring unanimity of the member states, and ratification by national Parliaments, or in some cases through referenda. Consequently we can rule out any such change, and in rejecting the theory on which the Treaty has been so foolishly based, reject the Treaty too.

So it is easy to see that bad economic policy is likely to be the outcome of EMU. There are two ways for bad policy to arise. One is that different areas need different policy and cannot have it, so someone has bad policy, or all have a compromise bad policy. Alternatively, the whole area may suffer from an excessively deflationary policy based on the disregard of any economic objective other than price stability.

Politically, poor economic performance is sure to reflect badly on the European ideal. Enthusiasm for European integration cannot possibly follow from economic failure created by EMU. But there is more to it than this simple fact. It is necessary to consider the case of a damaging policy being imposed from a foreign city. Imagine the scenario where inflation is a problem in Germany, France and some of the other countries. Interest rates rise, leading to a recession in one of the poorer countries which, let us suppose, did not have an inflation problem, and perhaps even needed lower interest rates. Most of the advocates of EMU, who are also hoping for closer political ties, apparently believe that using the same money will bind Europeans together more than the fact that rich countries will be seen to be imposing pointless recessions on poor ones will push them apart. The truth must be that such circumstances will lead to a growth of nationalist and perhaps even secessionist political movements in the recession-bound countries.

The fact that the governments of these countries are prohibited from seeking any mitigation of the harmful monetary policy can only make the problem worse. A policymaker who is seen to be accountable to the people of Europe as a whole might have a chance in such circumstances. One like the ECB, which will inevitably be seen as acting in the interest of the moneyed classes of the rich countries, will have none. It can lead only to the loss of legitimacy of European integration and in the extreme to the fragmentation of the Union.

So Maastricht means bad economic policy; this is anybody's case against the euro. But bad economic policy means bad economic outcomes, and when these are seen to be imposed from a foreign city, bad economics quickly becomes bad politics. This is the case for the liberals and internationalists, and those who have always welcomed European integration, to reject the euro.

2 The advantages of the euro

It is agreed on all sides that there are both costs and benefits of a group of countries sharing a currency. Most of the points that are frequently made either in favour of or against EMU could be made in the case of a proposal for a common currency for any group of countries. The balance of costs and benefits in each case would be different, but their basic character would be the same.

A large number of such benefits have been claimed for EMU. Most of them are ultimately traceable to the saving of costs in international transactions that a single currency brings. This is most obviously the case with the costs of trade, but the costs of dealing with exchange-rate uncertainty can be thought of in this way too. It has also been claimed that the euro will confer some international advantages on the European Union which are not simply the consequence of lower transactions costs. Offering a currency which can challenge the dollar in international markets is supposed to be one of these. Further, and much more speculative, claims have been made that eliminating these costs will itself lead to other gains, such as an improvement in the rate of economic growth on a permanent basis.

However, the economic costs of monetary unions are mainly traceable to the loss of the ability to set different monetary policies in different countries to reflect different conditions or preferences. It is in the nature of a monetary union that all parts of the union will share the same interest rates and the same exchange rate with the rest of the world. As the case of policymaking after German unification has illustrated, there will be circumstances when this forced uniformity is undesirable.

The essence of the case for EMU is the hope that the benefits outweigh the costs. It is possible that this is indeed the case for a small group of countries within the European Union: the most ardent Eurosceptic would not be sure that sharing a currency would harm Germany and the Netherlands. It is most unlikely, however, that there are net benefits for all the fifteen members, let alone the fifteen plus the countries of central and eastern Europe and others that are currently hoping to join the European Union.

As well as these arguments, which might apply with small changes to any monetary union, three other types of argument have been advanced in the European case. First, the European Commission says that 'the better formulation and implementation' of EU policies will bring benefits. However, its argument on this point simply consists of a wish-list of policy areas the Commission would like to control with no reason given for supposing they are linked with monetary union.[5]

Second, the euro is said to have political benefits. This important issue is considered in Chapter 6. The essential point is that if the euro is economically damaging, it is unlikely to promote harmony in the political sphere for long. The matter should therefore be debated in the first instance in terms of economic effects alone.

Third, it has been claimed that certain details of the institutional arrangements of the Maastricht Treaty give rise to extra benefits. In particular, the independent central bank and the Stability and Growth Pact are said to bring such benefits. This is a most serious mistake. These arrangements create an extra powerful argument against EMU and against British membership. Since these are costs, not benefits, they will be considered in Chapter 3.

The benefits of a single currency

Saving transactions costs

The most obvious benefit of a single currency is that some transactions costs in international business and travel can be eliminated, namely the cost of exchanging money when engaging in transactions ~~~~~~~~ member countries. Besides the benefit to those already i~

international transactions, there will be a few other individuals and companies who will be encouraged by the lower costs to engage in trade, so that there will also be an increase in the total volume of trade, presumably bringing some slight efficiency gain.

No one denies these benefits exist, but what of it? How important are they? The European Commission is far from being a disinterested party, but even its estimate puts the benefits at only 0.4 per cent of EU national income, with a concentration in the smaller and poorer countries.[6] A 0.4 per cent gain would mean that, on average, for every £100 we currently have, EMU brings an extra 40 pence. Since the United Kingdom is neither one of the smaller, such as Belgium or Ireland, nor one of the poorer countries, such as Greece or Portugal, the actual benefit might be as little as half of this, again according to the European Commission.

Even this figure needs to be treated with care. The benefit arises from the fact that certain functions no longer need to be performed. These are the functions of exchanging currencies in banks and bureaux de change around the continent and the related processing ones behind the scenes. The resources, mostly people, formerly employed to perform these functions can therefore, in principle, be employed in some other capacity. Society as a whole gains the benefit of the performance of that other function. This means that the cost saving identified by the European Commission must initially manifest itself as a loss of jobs in the banking sector, and presumably a loss of profitability in this sector as well. The benefit of monetary union arises only when the resources released from banking actually find alternative employment, which may take some time.

In connection with transactions costs, Christopher Huhne suggests that a study by Engel and Rogers of trade across the US–Canada border shows how important they are. These authors suggested that in a certain sense, taking goods across that border was equivalent to transporting them 1,780 miles.[7] Since Engel and Rogers' is a study from 1996, we should again be conscious that the growth of e-commerce, in which Britain leads Europe, should be expected to change their results dramatically. Even more importantly, however, the sample period of their study is September 1978 to December 1994. The end of it is, therefore, within the period of free trade between Canada and the United States, but most of it is not. Most importantly, even that agreement does not go nearly as far as the European Union's arrangements in the internal market. Therefore the impediments to trade across the US–Canada border include many things in addition to the effects (if any) of different currencies – namely all the things that the European Commission, and the British government of the time were rightly so keen to eliminate when the Single European Act, or '1992 Programme', was agreed. Finally, the peculiar fact that their measure of the impediment to trade increases once free trade begins clearly does not argue for the importance of a single currency. What it does is cast doubt on the validity of the study. No one should be fooled, then, by the attempts of the euro-advocates to pretend that one can infer a handicap to trade in Europe.

Transparency of pricing

Another benefit claimed by advocates of the euro is the so-called transparency of pricing. It is argued that having prices in a single currency will make it easier for consumers to compare them, and this will force prices down in the countries where they are currently highest, because otherwise people will simply import the goods in question from the country where they are cheapest. This view evidently presumes a considerable difficulty in comparing prices in different currencies. The use of the pocket calculator would therefore seem to be an alternative to the introduction of the euro, but furthermore, today, and increasingly in the future, currency conversion on internet sales-sites is clearly set to make price comparisons with anywhere in the world a matter of ease. The argument for the euro is already being left behind by technology.

The euro-advocates' favourite example of this used to be the case of cars in Britain allegedly costing more than in continental Europe. Here, the important thing to remember is that the argument being made is not merely that cars are more expensive in the UK than elsewhere, but that this is specifically because competitive pressures are prevented from operating by the fact that consumers have difficulty in comparing prices. Nothing but this establishes the importance of transparency. Yet numerous other explanations of high car prices are available. The European Commission itself said, when advocating the Single Market, that price differences were caused by the Commission's own rules, and the 'trading practices of the leading manufacturers'. No mention was made of the possibility that the existence of different currencies had anything to do with it. And indeed, in 2000, the Competition Commission investigated the matter and reported finding 'a complex monopoly situation'.[8] The clearest refutation of the case, however, comes from the fact that the issue of car prices has been in the news so often and for so long, and indeed it has been reiterated ad nauseam by the euro-advocates to such an extent that it boggles the mind that people allegedly remain ignorant of the price difference. Yet if the difference persists when people know about it, it cannot be a problem of price transparency.

Reducing exchange-rate uncertainty

A third alleged source of benefit from a single currency is the elimination of costs associated with uncertainty about future exchange rates. For example, if a firm is contemplating an investment which will ultimately produce revenue from a foreign country, it may be inhibited by the fact that it does not know what that revenue will later be worth in terms of its own currency. This introduces an element of risk into any such investment. If this risk poses a serious problem to a sufficiently large number of firms, efficient financial markets might be expected to be able to eliminate it, although of course they would charge a fee. In this case the fee is the cost of the exchange-rate uncertainty. The fact that firms cannot generally purchase this kind of insurance must to some degree suggest that there is not much demand for it. This, in turn, suggests that the perceived risks are not all that great.

A consideration which is absolutely crucial, however, albeit one which is routinely ignored by the advocates of the euro, is that exchange-rate certainty comes at a cost of uncertainty of other kinds. It is a sad fact that the advocates of the euro have fallen completely into the caricature of the economist whose favourite assumption is that 'other things are equal'. As will be argued in Chapter 3, the crucial thing that will not be the same is that the loss of national policy will reduce the predictability of unemployment, and even inflation, in each country. A greater certainty of exchange rates combined with more uncertainty about the likely level of demand for a product is hardly calculated to inspire in businesses the kind of confidence which will lead to a long-term increase in investment.

Even considering the issue of exchange-rate uncertainty alone, the argument is more problematic than it seems. One issue is the effect of the introduction of the euro on the unpredictability of exchange rates between Europe and the rest of the world. Should this increase, there will be losses to firms trading outside the euro area.

In this case, it has been argued that the evidence of the period of the gold standard shows how great the advantages of the elimination of risk are. The analysis is defective however, because there are other important factors affecting those countries in that period. At that time, huge investment opportunities were opening up in countries which had little capital of their own. Those opportunities were naturally financed from the 'old world'. The fact that Canada and Australia attracted the most investment makes the point rather clearly: one should not suppose that the gold standard is the explanation for people taking advantage of opportunities in those countries in the period after 1880.[9]

Another academic study, by Professor Rose (2000), has received some attention. His headline-worthy finding was that after a number of statistical techniques were used, countries which share a currency trade with each other something like three times as much as they would if they had different currencies. This study has attracted criticism over its statistical approach, as well as over whether the countries treated as having the same currency in fact do so. It is also most notable that the majority of monetary unions he discovers are between one large country and very small ones. Whether this is the explanation of his result is uncertain. What is clear, however, is that the advocates of the euro will have to be very careful about adopting his study for their cause – there is certainly no sign as yet that the volume of trade in Europe is set to treble.

It should be noted finally that in so far as there are, in normal circumstances, benefits in exchange-rate stability, nothing prohibits Britain or any other country outside the euro from pursuing a policy designed to stabilise its exchange rate. This has for some time been the policy of Denmark, where the krone has be held in a fairly narrow band with respect to the Deutschmark (or euro). In the referendum there, the advocates of the euro argued that this meant nothing would be lost by joining. But it was more persuasively argued that nothing much would be gained, whilst what would be lost is the ability to change the exchange rate should future circumstances so demand. It is in the light of this that arguments about the volubility of the pound in recent years should be seen. The most it shows is that more attention should be paid to the stabilisation of the exchange rate as one aspect of a balanced policy.

Challenging the dollar

Creating a currency which can 'rival the dollar' has been one of the long-standing goals of many continental policymakers, although it has never been entirely clear what it means. If it is really a matter of international prestige or 'giving the European Union a monetary identity', we should be cautious as to whether any real benefit exists.

Another possibility is that it is anticipated that the euro will displace the dollar as the currency of pricing of internationally traded goods such as oil. At present, wherever in the world oil is traded it is priced in dollars. It is difficult to see that any great national advantage accrues to the United States. Everybody has to pay the same amount whatever currency the prices are quoted in. And if there is some advantage, why would the creation of the euro cause the Americans or anyone else to change the way oil is priced?

Much the same thinking applies to British companies which have announced that they intend to keep certain accounts in euros rather than pounds. They are free to think in whatever currency they like, but nothing material is affected by the decision, and their practices in this regard have no bearing on whether it is beneficial to the country as a whole to adopt the use of a different currency and accept having its monetary policy made abroad.

A slightly more serious idea is that at present the United States gains a benefit from the fact that non-Americans hold dollars rather than their own currency. As a result the US government has what is in effect an interest-free loan. Similar, although smaller, benefits have accrued to European governments, but it is hoped that the euro will play a larger role of this kind.

One aspect of this consideration is that it has been suggested that the issuance of a €500 note will be useful to criminals around the world, since large amounts of money can be transported easily in this form without having to go through the banking system. It is an unlikely thought that the European Union wishes to be in the business of lubricating the illegal and drug-related activities of the world's mafia by offering them a more convenient store of value than the dollar, but it has to be admitted that, disreputable as it is, a small financial benefit may result.

Although such effects, if they occur, might be counted as a benefit by some, this would still be a difficult area for advocates of the euro. The Bundesbank regarded the accumulation of Deutschmarks abroad as disadvantageous for Germany because it put the Bundesbank in danger of losing control of the German money supply. On this basis challenging the dollar would be seen as a disadvantage.

Lower interest rates

One of the favourite arguments of many of the advocates of the euro has been that it would lead to lower interest rates in Britain. This can mean two rather different things. The first is that short-term interest rates would be lower. That would, for example, make variable-rate mortgage payments lower. Since all countries in a monetary union share the same short-term interest rate, and euro-area rates have been below British ones, this is true. It is quite certain, however, that it would have been a great cost for Britain. This is because short-term interest rates are a principal tool of economic management. For the last few years British rates have been higher than continental ones. This is because the Bank of England, charged with controlling inflation, has set them there. They could certainly have set them lower, but have not done so for the good reason that they believe it would cause inflation.

It is therefore a rather poor performance by the euro-advocates to keep on attempting to lure mortgage-payers into their net with this promise of lower interest rates. If they wish to criticise the Bank of England for having made a misjudgement of British conditions and set interest rates too high, they should do so straightforwardly. If they do not take that course, advocating the euro on the basis that it will result in lower rates is merely to admit that those rates would be inappropriate, and a perfect way to return to a boom and bust cycle.

The case of long-term interest rates is rather different. These are essentially determined by financial markets, and policymakers have much less direct influence. It is usual to suppose that as long as the ultimate ability of the borrower to repay a loan is not in question – and in the case of government debt it tends not to be – these rates are determined by the market's expectation of inflation. If it is anticipated that inflation will be high, naturally one does not lend at a low rate of interest since the repayment is going to be devalued by the inflation. It has been more or less an article of faith of the advocates of the euro that British long-term interest rates are always bound to be higher than euro-area ones. The explanation of this view lies in some ill-specified argument that it is forever impossible for British policymakers to con-vince the financial markets that inflation here will be controlled. Since the creation of the euro, however, British long-term rates have fallen below continental ones. This is despite the fact that the stated objective of British policymakers is that inflation be stabilised at 2.5 per cent whereas the European Central Bank has announced that it will seek to keep inflation 'below 2 per cent'. So the markets must be presumed to have considerably more confidence in the British policymakers than they do in the euro-area ones. Since the advocates of the euro have been in the habit of placing much stress on the question of long-term interest rates, this development evidently leaves their argument in dis-array.

An increase in mergers?

Christopher Huhne notes that there has been a great increase in the number of mergers in the euro zone in the last few years, and fears that Britain is missing out on some benefit in that area. Three questions arise here: whether these mergers are in fact beneficial; whether they are caused by the euro; and whether mergers would be increasing in Britain in the same way if we had joined. On the first issue the answer can be none too clear. There is some element of fashion and jumping on the bandwagon about many of these mergers and whether they will turn out to add value only time will tell.

As to whether they are really caused by the euro, there must be a great deal of doubt. Continental Europe has not had the tradition of corporate governance that has prevailed in the Anglo-Saxon world and it can well be argued that the case of the Vodafone–Mannesmann take-over has created a cultural shift, and that it is this which is causing the increase in mergers.

Similarly, the rate of hostile takeovers having been so much higher in the UK than in continental Europe for so long, one must wonder whether Britain is in fact missing out on anything. The picture looks rather more like Europe simply catching up with the way things are done here. If that is, in fact, attributable to the euro, it may be good news, but it would still not be relevant to the British decision: We have nothing to gain (or lose) from this consideration, because we already have that financial culture.

Effects on the rate of growth

A further argument sometimes advanced is that there will be an increase in the euro area's rate of growth. It is said that the gains already considered will increase output in the euro area, and some of this extra output will be invested. If this happens the capital stock grows faster than it otherwise would have and thus increases output further, yielding additional benefits in the form of a faster rate of growth. These are sometimes called 'dynamic' gains. By this argument the advocates of the euro hope to show that small initial benefits can, over time, through the working of compound growth rates, turn into worthwhile amounts of money. Indeed, it is true that if a policy can be devised which will increase the rate of growth, even by a fraction of 1 per cent, large gains will eventually result.

However, to treat this point as a further argument for the euro is an elementary mistake of logic. A crucial assumption is that the basic effects of the euro are to increase output. This is the essential foundation on which dynamic gains are built. But before it can be determined whether this increase in output exists, it is necessary to consider both the costs and the benefits of the euro, not just the benefits. It cannot be argued that the savings in transactions costs will generate extra investment, and that this will bring a dynamic benefit, if the issue of the dynamic costs associated with the harmful effects of the euro is then ignored. On the assumption that these dynamic effects exist – something which tends to be assumed by supporters of the euro – we face a potentially disastrous outcome. First, bad economic performance lowers output; that lowers investment, bringing a further fall in output, and even less investment. The mistake of supposing that dynamic effects can exist only on the benefit side was made by the

European Commission and has unfortunately been followed by almost all who have written on the matter since. Nevertheless, it is obviously an error.

So dynamic effects should not feature at all in a discussion of whether the euro is desirable. Once this issue has been settled, dynamic effects may change the size of the overall cost or benefit. But then the power of compound growth might just as well be working against the euro as in its favour, and it takes only a small negative effect on the growth rate for the dynamic consequences for Europe to be disastrous.

Similar points may be made in relation to other claims that are made for the euro. For example, an old standby of the European Commission is the survey of business opinion. When business opinion is favourable to the Commission's proposals, much is made of the fact that the increased confidence will promote investment.[10] But, again, a favourable opinion cannot be expected to be maintained if the consequences turn out to be negative, and then presumably the same line of argument suggests a dramatic fall in investment.

On the benefit side, therefore, we have very little. The benefits of transparency of prices is an illusion; exchange-rate stability is a benefit only granted the 'other things equal' sleight of hand; having lower short-term interest rates forced on us – whether they are described as 'business finance' or 'mortgage' rates – would be an own-goal disrupting our proper economic management; having European long-term interest rates could cost us billions; mergers in Britain need no encouragement from the euro; dynamic effects are not benefits at all, but simply a factor magnifying either the costs or benefits that emerge from all the other factors – good and bad – together. There is still the 20 pence in every £100, at least according to the European Commission's estimates, but that is really it.

3 The disadvantages of the euro

O n the cost side, it is important to distinguish between costs which would arise from any introduction of a single currency in an area the size of the European Union and those which arise specifically from the details of the Maastricht Treaty. The overwhelming effort of the euro advocates has gone into arguing that the European Union would benefit from a single currency, and it is important that the deficiencies of these arguments are appreciated. But there has been comparatively little effort to address the serious deficiencies of the Maastricht Treaty, which is not only economically dangerous but also threatens to undermine the political fabric of Europe. This chapter will consider the costs of any single currency and then the details of the Maastricht Treaty.

PART 1 THE COSTS OF A SINGLE CURRENCY

The costs of changeover

There is no denying that the clearest cost of the euro – although not, I shall argue, anything like the largest – is that of simply changing from one currency to the other. There must be some doubt as to whether the benefits, such as they are, would even cover this cost. Estimates were made by chartered accountants Chantrey Vellacott DFK. They suggested the cost of changeover for Britain would be about £36 billion – something like 4 per cent of national output. These estimates have been criticised by the advocates of the euro, and no doubt they are not perfect, but they should not be dismissed. The House of Commons Trade and Industry Select Committee has been concerned about conversion costs, and in a report of 2000 specifically noted the Chantrey

Vellacott study and said in their conclusion, 'the information that we have received from disparate organisations does not suggest that high estimates have been inflated.' They also deplored the lack of attention that has been given to the issue and cast doubt on the view that it had even been properly assessed on the Continent.[11]

The difficulty is that the euro-advocates seem rather reluctant to have a proper costing undertaken by the government. Although in the modern world it is routine to expect both governments and oppositions to cost their proposals, in this case it seems to be supposed that the rules should be rather different. It is particularly notable that so many euro-advocate politicians in parties ostensibly committed to debate and to openness of government decline to join in calls for a proper government costing. This complacency about how great the costs are is even more surprising when set beside remarks of Lord Simon – the government minister responsible for the euro. He expressed alarm that too few firms had made preparations for the euro at all.[12] But their reluctance, and his concern, both point to the fact that time and money are required. Therefore, if the advocates of the euro do not like the estimates of the costs that are available, they need to be responsible enough to produce some of their own. The conclusion of the Trade and Industry Select Committee still rings in the ears of those who would have a proper debate of issues: 'Fear of producing high figures cannot be a barrier to thorough and informed consideration of the likely costs of the changeover period.'[13]

The costs of common policy

The important cost of a single currency is that all parts of the monetary union must have the same monetary and exchange-rate policy at all times. Clearly, if Germany and Spain have the same currency, the exchange rate between the Spanish currency and the dollar and the Germany currency and the dollar must be the same. Similarly, interest rates must be the same in both countries. The case would be the same as in the United States. Interest rates cannot be systematically lower in New

York than in California, simply because nothing prevents a Californian borrowing in New York and lending in California, if this is advantageous. Any such transcontinental borrowing would itself tend to lead to an equalisation of interest rates through the market mechanism.

Interest-rate differences may exist when there are separate currencies because in this case, even in the absence of legal restrictions on foreign borrowing, people are aware of the dangers of changes in currency values. In 2000 a European could borrow at lower interest rates in Japan than anywhere in the euro area. But when the time comes to repay the loan, the number of euros owed will depend on how the exchange rate has changed in the interim. Presumably, it is this danger that has deterred large numbers of Europeans from borrowing in yen. This factor does not exist within a currency union and there is therefore no impediment to the equalisation of interest rates.

There are three cases where it will be disadvantageous to have the same interest rates everywhere. The most frequently discussed is that of non-synchronous business cycles. This is sometimes called the problem of asymmetric shocks, with a shock being anything which causes either a boom or a recession. It is asymmetric if different countries suffer different shocks, or some suffer none at all. In such a case higher interest rates could be called for in one country whereas lower ones are needed in another. A particularly clear example of the desirability of separate interest rates is offered by the different developments of the British and continental economies through the latter part of the 1990s. Britain recovered from a bad recession at the beginning of the decade, and by the late 1990s was in more danger of inflation than recession. Continental Europe was for a long time stuck in recession. No interest rate could have been set that would be appropriate to both. There are relatively few among the advocates of the euro who still own up to having wanted Britain to join in the 'first wave', but many of them did. The idea that it would have been anything other than disastrous is absurd.

An illustration of the difficulties Britain would now be in is offered by Ireland. There, a decision was taken to join despite the fact that the

Irish economy was, even well before the final decisions were taken, showing signs of boom. Irish interest rates were cut to continental levels, and the boom has grown worse. For the time being, it seems easy to take a relaxed attitude to this, indeed, one might even wonder how the euro can be a problem if it causes a fall in unemployment, a rise in house and share prices and a general surge of confidence. And it is possible even to fall into the trap of thinking that some rise in inflation might be a price worth paying for this.

All of this is a great mistake, and the danger lies in what comes next. While prices are rising faster in Ireland than they are in the rest of the euro area, if other things are equal, Irish firms are losing international competitiveness. Their costs, many of which are wages and rents paid in Ireland, will be rising faster than those elsewhere. For the time being this may do little harm because confidence and demand in Ireland itself are so high. In the longer term, however, it must result in an erosion of their position in international markets. In due course this will bring the boom to an end, and when that happens, it will be painfully obvious that the inflation which has accumulated in the interim poses a critical problem. Irish firms will have lost international competitiveness and face a domestic market in recession.

Before EMU, such an outcome could have been avoided. Irish interest rates could have risen when the boom was first perceived, and this would have helped to prevent it. If, nevertheless it occurred, it would then be possible to both cut interest rates to stimulate recovery, and allow the exchange rate to fall to restore international competitiveness. Unfortunately, in monetary union, none of these things is possible. The only way that competitiveness can be restored is by forcing wages and prices to fall in Ireland relative to those in the rest of the euro area. On the assumption – which is usually a key component of the case for the euro – that euro-area prices will be stable, this means Irish wages and prices must fall. It will be interesting to see how that is achieved, but to imagine it happening without a sustained, painful and damaging period of unemployment is very optimistic.

Furthermore, it is worth noting that the Irish case, in certain respects, understates the danger. One consequence of the Irish boom has been some immigration, mostly of Irish expatriates returning home. That works in the direction of limiting wage increases and inflation. Other countries, however, do not have such a large pool of expatriate labour to call on, and in similar circumstances, they can expect the inflationary consequences to be worse.

The key point, then, is that all problems of divergence within the euro area are ultimately problems of unemployment. They may initially manifest themselves as excessive inflation, but that will produce a loss of competitiveness, and in time, an end to inflation and a loss of jobs. It should be remembered in thinking about loss of competitiveness that inflation differentials are cumulative: if our inflation is 2 per cent higher than the rest this year, and next year, that is a 4 per cent loss. If business profit margins are only 10–20 per cent of price, then it takes very little to create a serious problem. The fact that these problems manifest themselves only when the local boom has dissipated is a poor reason for ignoring them.

Indeed this point has been made rather well by Romano Prodi, the President of the European Commission, discussing the very much milder predicament that Italy is in. He said, 'We have had a very low inflation, only 2 per cent, but other European competitors have had 1 per cent. If our costs diverge and we continue on this road we will fail to remain in the euro. To lose one point a year in competitiveness over a period of time would be a tragedy.'[14]

The second key point is that the problem arises because of the unavoidability of sharing interest rates with countries in a different position, and the impossibility of changing the exchange rate. And third, the same fate could easily have befallen Britain, had we joined the euro. Furthermore, we would have joined – and suffered – if those who imagine the issue is just a political one and want to see Britain 'at the top table' or 'at the heart of Europe' or whatever their current phrase may be, had had their way.

THE ARGUMENTS AGAINST THE EURO

One might try to explain away the Irish case as a consequence of their catching up with the rest of Europe in terms of economic standard of living. In theory, that might work, although it remains an optimistic view. Some slight inflation might be appropriate, but for the Irish inflation to be as high as it is can only be a serious problem. Furthermore, one must take note of the concern now being expressed in the European Union about Ireland. The Commission has been attempting to instruct the Irish on their tax policy in such a way as to bring this boom to an end.[15] So if there is in fact no economic problem, this would have to be seen as a pure attempt to interfere with national self-government – something the euro-advocates usually deny will happen.

To many – including, it seems, the European Commission – Ireland appears to be in the inflationary stage of such a disaster. If she escapes through some fortunate circumstance, everyone will be pleased. But no one should imagine that it shows the problem doesn't exist. What remains the inescapable fact is that we have an illustration of the dangers the euro brings – dangers to jobs and prosperity. An inflation like that in Ireland – like the one that would have occurred in the UK had we joined at the outset – would still be a horrible price to pay for a piece of political symbolism, and far more expensive than the 20 pence in £100 pounds we give up by not joining.

In addition to the case in which business cycles are out of sequence – the same kind of problem can arise in two other ways. One is when different countries respond at different speeds to similar developments. So, if one thinks of something like a sustained, large increase in commodity prices, which might initially seem to affect everyone in the same kind of way, differential responses to the initial effect will lead to a divergence of interest in just the same way as if the initial cause had been different. The second is the possibility of different countries having different preferences about how to respond to conditions. One consequence of the euro is that such freedom is given up

In each of these examples the policy ends up being a compromise of some kind. A small country such as Ireland will more or less have the continent's preferences imposed on it. A larger one may influence the choice of policy, but then the policy serves no interest fully. This is the basic cost of a single currency, whether in Europe or elsewhere.

The benefits of exchange rate changes

A common element of these situations is that in the absence of monetary union they are likely to be met with different interest rates, which will lead to exchange-rate changes. It has been a theme of the advocacy of monetary union that exchange-rate changes cannot bring any benefits beyond, perhaps, the short run. Thus Emerson *et al.*[16] say that after an initial benefit from devaluation 'import prices work through into consumption prices. These price increases will sooner or later feed through in nominal wages and therefore in domestic output prices', so that in the longer term devaluation causes only inflation.

This certainly appears to be true of some devaluations, such as those of the franc in 1981 and 1983. Others, however, have been highly successful. Most obvious among these is the British exit from the ERM in 1992, which clearly restarted growth. Although opponents of devaluation at the time were convinced that there would be high inflation within a year or two, they were wrong. Nor is this exceptional; Belgium enjoyed a successful devaluation in 1982, as did Mexico in 1994. Indeed, even the French devaluations of 1958 and 1969 were successful. The interesting question is why some devaluations are successful and others are not.

It is easy to see the effects of a devaluation in a country with full employment as inflationary. The devaluation improves the competitiveness of both exporting and import-competing firms by reducing the amount of foreign currency required to pay a price fixed in the domestic currency. When the pound was devalued each Deutschmark bought more pounds, so from the German point of view British exports became cheaper. Similarly, from the British point of view more pounds were needed to purchase imports.

These effects have two inflationary tendencies. One is that imports cost more. Whether these are final goods or inputs to production, the price to consumers in the devaluing country will generally be higher. The other is that the improvement in competitiveness will increase employment, and this too will push in the direction of higher wages and hence higher costs and prices. If, as assumed, the devaluing country has full employment, an increase in inflation must be expected. There is a greater demand for labour but few unemployed workers. Presumably there was already buoyant consumer demand and retailers will feel free to raise prices. If the devaluation also comes at a time of expansionary government policy, as it may since this policy may be the reason for the low level of unemployment, there is further reason to expect a rapid price increase.

The case is different for a country that has been pursuing an anti-inflation policy but finds its currency overvalued, perhaps because of past inflation. The country will be experiencing a recession and unemployment will presumably be rather high because of the anti-inflationary policy and because the past inflation will have put domestic firms at a competitive disadvantage. It is reasonable to hope that the improved competitiveness following a devaluation will result in a fall in unemployment, and that prices will be slower to rise. The devaluation still creates some tendency to inflation, but this simply shows why successful devaluations have tended not only to occur with unemployment rather high, but have also been accompanied by continued disinflationary policy.

Confusion arises because advocates of the euro speak as if the successful outcome of the British devaluation of 1992 was merely a piece of luck. They imply that recession, lack of consumer confidence, the high level of unemployment and the continued government policy of bearing down on inflation were just a fortunate coincidence. The truth is that it is precisely such circumstances which make devaluation an appropriate weapon. No one would have been advocating a devaluation had these not been the circumstances. Similar situations may be expected to arise in some part of the European Union fairly frequently. If the circumstances are right and the accompanying policies are appropriate there is no reason all devaluations should not be successful.

Advocates of the euro are also inclined to assert that most British devaluations have led only to inflation and that there has been some sort of vicious circle at work. The record since the Second World War is as follows. In 1949 there was a general European devaluation against the dollar in which Britain played a leading role, but which involved the whole continent. It did much to balance the post-war world economy, and there was no appreciable inflation subsequently. Next came a highly successful devaluation in 1967. Some years later there was a major inflation, the 'Barber boom', but, despite the attempts of certain of the euro-advocates to rewrite history in order to merge the two events together, this was caused by a quite separate mishandling of policy by a later government of a different party. In 1971 there was a general realignment of the Bretton Woods system, again not focusing on Britain. The major feature was a devaluation of the dollar, and the value of the pound increased in dollar terms. In 1972 Britain left the European snake and the pound floated (downwards). This occurred in inflationary conditions and would not be expected to bring any benefits: this one case roughly fits the alleged general pattern. Lastly, in 1992, there was the exit from the EMS and another float, which has been extremely successful.

It is also worth remembering that while one country may need to devalue, others will simultaneously benefit from their currency moving upwards. It is another fallacy beloved of the euro-advocates that the only motive one could have for preserving a separate currency is to keep the freedom to devalue. Of course this is rubbish: what is at stake is the freedom to manage one's economy, including the exchange rate, appropriately to conditions. Indeed, 1992 again affords a good example. In the period immediately before the pound's exit from the ERM, the Bundesbank allowed it to be known that it favoured a devaluation of the pound. It is safe to assume that the Bundesbank's interest in the matter was in achieving an upward valuation of the Deutschmark to reduce inflation in Germany rather than a concern for the management of the British economy. But of course anything which would have prevented the pound devaluing would have prevented the desired rise in the value of the Deutschmark as well. EMU would have hurt both countries.

Recent British experience affords another example. In response to a booming economy and the policy that has accompanied it, the pound has risen. It seems impossible to deny that a beneficial effect of this is that it has helped to keep inflation down. It is true, of course, that some firms are hurt by the level of the pound, but they would not be favoured for long if the level of the pound were fixed (in the euro or any other way) and their international competitiveness destroyed by British inflation.[17]

There is a related point that is frequently made, namely that the rather spectacular fall in the value of the euro in the couple of years after its launch is beneficial because it helps continental Europe out of its recession. It seems to me that this is certainly correct, at least up to a point. But I am at a loss to explain the adoption of the argument by the advocates of the euro. If they believe that exchange rate changes are useful, then the case is closed: the euro is a bad idea.

What can be done in a monetary union?

The problems which lead to the need for a different policy might not occur. Policy preferences might not differ. Indeed, it is clear that most policymakers currently believe that the control of inflation should always be the overriding priority. However, this view is unlikely to persist for ever, particularly if some countries seem to be doing much better out of the policy than others. It might also be hoped that responses to similar circumstances will also be similar, or at least will progressively become more similar if the euro exists for long enough. No doubt various proposals could be produced for speeding the process. Nevertheless, it needs to be appreciated that in so far as they are not the same at present, or that there are costs involved in making them more similar, these things are costs of the euro project.

When problems do arise a possibility is that fiscal changes – that is, changes in taxation and government expenditure – could soften the blow of harmful monetary policy. Where part of the monetary union is experiencing a boom and interest rates cannot rise because other countries are in recession, taxes might be increased to try to stop the boom. Thus in the case of Ireland joining the euro with its economy growing unsustainably quickly, a sufficient increase in taxation might, by cutting off the boom, prevent any great problem arising. The opposite case of a country in recession while the rest of the monetary union needs interest rates to rise is rather more difficult in the European case. In principle, taxes could be cut and government expenditure increased to combat the recession. However, the Maastricht Treaty and subsequent agreements place limits on the level of government borrowing, so this avenue is largely closed off. This is a particularly foolish aspect of the Treaty which will be considered at more length in Part 2 of this chapter.

This asymmetry is one of the reasons there is every danger of the euro being recession-prone. Booming countries can deal with this problem by raising taxes, but the ability of recession-bound countries to take the appropriate fiscal action is severely restricted. On average we must therefore expect a more significant problem with recession than boom.

An alternative would exist if the European Union had power to tax and spend sufficiently large amounts in each country. Then it could reduce the damage from a common monetary policy by taxing booming regions and spending the money in countries in recession. This is one of the things central governments do when different regions of one country experience different conditions; indeed, the effect arises largely automatically from the operation of the tax and benefit systems. In the EU the central budget is too small and too specifically committed to agriculture to operate in this way, although the possibility that this will change will be considered in Chapter 5.

Another theoretical possibility is that unemployed labour might migrate from one country to wherever there are jobs. The United States functions effectively as a monetary union, despite the fact that different areas have non-synchronous business cycles, largely because many people are willing to move across the country if necessary. (The claim that they are moving for the weather has no evidence in its support. Are we to believe that these migrations would take place if there were no jobs to go to?) There are obvious difficulties with this in the European Union because of language and other cultural barriers, so labour is much less mobile. Thus the alleviation of the problem through this route will be negligible.

Another difficult, although unaddressed, issue is that of the extent to which it will be politically acceptable for economic sacrifices to be required of one part of a monetary union in the interests of other parts. Even in the United States, there are resentments when one part of the country feels that interest rates are being raised because of inflationary pressures in other parts. But the United States is a well-established nation state. Along with these resentments there is also a deeper acceptance that this is the way policy must be set. The same largely applies in the United Kingdom. East Anglia may suffer from British policy, but people in East Anglia do not give the impression that they feel the way policy is determined lacks political legitimacy or infringes their rights.

But what of the south of Italy and Germany? Or Greece, now that it has decided to join, and the industrial centre of Europe? What of Ireland, even, and the rest of the euro area? At some point circumstances will arise where lower interest rates are required in one of the poorer countries than are forthcoming from the central bankers in Frankfurt. Are we to suppose that the central policymaking apparatus of the European Union has sufficient political legitimacy for this to be acceptable in whichever country is suffering? In many ways, this may be the most dangerous aspect of the whole experiment.

It is for this reason that Christopher Huhne's Table 4.1 (p59 of the reverse part of this book) and his arguments about correlation coefficients among different European countries and different regions of the United States are beside the point. They aim to demonstrate that there is about the same tendency for economic performance to diverge among European regions as among parts of existing countries, so that, on the face of it, there is about the same need for separate policy. But a divergence between two European countries sharing the same currency is far more serious than a divergence within a culturally and politically more homogeneous area such as an established nation state, which is also operating a reasonable national fiscal policy.

So, as a theoretical possibility, it could be that the costs of having a common currency in Europe may never manifest themselves. However, even on the basis of the arguments in this section, the risks are great. In the likely case of a boom in one place and recession in the other, the euro area will face an unsolvable policy problem. Whatever action is taken, the results will fall well short of those that could be achieved with separate currencies. It is reasonable to question how often such divergences of interest will arise, and whether the government's economic tests do not protect us against this kind of problem. The government has said after all, that there will be no question of joining until we are sure that our convergence will be sustainable.

Such optimism is, however, misplaced. A temporary convergence might well be achieved, but it is in the nature of the thing that future developments remain unpredictable, and nothing guarantees that at some point in the future there will not be a need for different policies. Indeed, such an outcome at some point in the future is a virtual certainty. Therefore, there is no serious prospect of any observable development guaranteeing a permanent convergence. It should be remembered that the euro countries themselves went through a process of convergence after Maastricht. It was rather painful and lasted at least from the agreement until 1999, and one might say that it really began earlier. A ten-year process of convergence, however, did not work for long. By early March 1999, just ten *weeks* into the life of the euro, the President of the ECB was complaining that different circumstances around the area made 'evaluation and judgement more difficult. Developments in parts of the euro zone seem to be diverging.' If such an admission can be forthcoming so early, it is clear that there can never be a guarantee of sustained convergence.[18]

The economic case for a single currency in Europe, then, is the case for risking a large amount for a small gain, with almost a certainty of losing.

PART 2 THE DANGERS OF THE MAASTRICHT PLAN

The Maastricht Plan is, however, much more than just a plan for a common currency. It also contains a blueprint for how economic policy is to be conducted within the monetary union. For this reason, the issues considered in the previous section are far from being the only ones of importance. The issue of monetary union cannot be treated simply as a matter of whether Europe would or would not be well served by a single currency.

The problem with the Maastricht Treaty is that it prohibits the implementation of good economic policy. It does this in various ways. First, it creates a central bank to run policy over which no other body is to have any influence, and it requires it to give absolute priority to price stability irrespective of the consequences. Second, it imposes arbitrary and foolish rules limiting the ability of the governments of the member states to use policies of taxation and expenditure to pursue the other fundamental objectives of economic policy: employment and growth. Third, it pretends that good policy is simply a matter of making rules to be administered by technicians and that political accountability has no role in economic policy in democracies.

Although these rules threaten economic prosperity in Europe and indeed possibly the world, it does not follow that the objectives of the Treaty – low inflation and limited government indebtedness – are themselves undesirable. It is a question of how these objectives should be achieved, and how their achievement interacts with the achievement of other objectives. The presumptions behind the Maastricht Treaty are that, notwithstanding great evidence to the contrary, they are easily achieved, and that, again in contradiction of the facts, they automatically bring with them the achievement of all other goals. The truth is much closer to the opposite: rules like those of the Maastricht Treaty have been tried and they do not work. Such rules do not bring prosperity, they bring economic failure.

The theoretical presumptions of the Maastricht Treaty are that the central bank's policy has no significant effects on employment beyond short periods of time; that the European Union need concern itself only with its domestic objective of price stability and can ignore issues of economic performance in the rest of the world; and that good fiscal policy is achieved by discipline and firmness rather than by a proper understanding of the relationship between the government's taxation and expenditure decisions and the behaviour of the private sector.

First, it is important to see what the Maastricht Treaty says. Next, the rationale which is given for the provisions of the Treaty can be considered. Then it will be argued that the theoretical presumptions are wrong, and indeed that this has been demonstrated by recent European experience.

What the Treaty says

The Maastricht Treaty deals with much more than monetary union. It covers citizenship, consumer protection, the environment, policing and many other matters. But these things have all been agreed; there is no British opt-out from them. Only the issue of the British membership of EMU remains to be settled, and this is what is considered here.

The independence of the European Central Bank

It is clear that the adoption of a single currency means that there must be a single central bank, replacing the separate central banks such as the Bundesbank and the Bank of France and, potentially, the Bank of England. This single central bank takes over the function of controlling interest rates.

It has become fashionable in many countries to take the view that monetary policy is best carried out by a central bank which is 'independent'. However, independence means different things in different countries. For example, in the United States, the Federal Reserve System is in certain respects independent of presidential and congressional control; but it is statutorily required to pursue a variety of objectives and in practice its obligation to report to Congress, and its desire to avoid prolonged conflicts with the Presidential administration, mean that it typically pursues a fairly balanced policy. But in the European Union, the Treaty categorically rejects the view that there should be any democratic input into monetary policymaking at all. Article 107 of the Treaty says:

> Neither the ECB nor a national central bank, nor any member of their decision-making bodies shall seek or take instructions from Community institutions or bodies, from any government of a Member State or from any other body. The Community institutions and bodies and the governments of the Member States undertake to respect this principle and not to seek to influence the members of the decision-making bodies of the ECB or of the national central banks.

So although other independent central banks are quite clearly under the control of elected governments in important ways, such as having their targets set for them by the government, or at least being ultimately subject to legislation, the European Central Bank (ECB) is to be protected by international treaty, even from attempts to influence it. This is a remarkable departure for the European Union, which is an organisation supposedly committed to the principles of democracy, and it is surprising that the formulation of Article 107 has not attracted more attention.

Comparing this with the present position in Britain, no one should imagine the two are equivalent. The crucial difference is that here, together with the move towards independence, there has also been careful attention to the accountability of the Bank of England to the elected government and also to that government's right to set the objective of the central bank. Whether even this kind of independence is desirable is debatable, but it is certainly not the gross breach of democratic principles entailed by the Maastricht Treaty. Nor is the British case exceptional. Even in Germany there was no legal provision which went as far as the Maastricht Treaty.

So the Treaty is no simple reflection of the fashion for central bank independence. It is a far more extreme version, and one which denies even the ultimate accountability of the central bank to the people. As we shall see, when combined with the objective which the ECB has been given and the difficulty of changing the Treaty, this independence is not just objectionable, but dangerous.

The objective of price stability

The ECB, besides being made independent, has been given an unchangeable objective, that of achieving price stability. Again the wording of the Maastricht Treaty is remarkably clear. Referring to the ESCB (the European System of Central Banks), meaning the ECB itself as well as all the national central banks, Article 105 of the Treaty says:

> The primary objective of the ESCB shall be to maintain price sta-
> bility. Without prejudice to the objective of price stability, it shall
> support the general economic policies of the Community with a
> view to contributing to the achievement of the objectives of the
> Community

It is a remarkable characteristic of this part of the Treaty that price stability had been made the overriding objective. Other objectives are considered, but it is explicit and clear that they are secondary and may be pursued only when price stability is secure. Given a conflict between economic growth and price stability, or employment and price stability, or, indeed, any measure of prosperity and price stability, prosperity comes second and price stability first.

It is sometimes said in defence of the Treaty that the national governments maintain power over whether to join an exchange-rate system, and that this would in practice give them the power to control interest rates. If it is interest rates that control inflation, then they have, by the back door, a way to overrule the central bank. Whatever the theoretical merits of this view, it is immaterial since there is no prospect of there being an exchange-rate system for Europe to join. Another possibility, allowed for in Article 109, is that the national governments may formulate 'general orientations for exchange-rate policy'. This too might seem to give a route to influencing the exchange rate. However, the same article says that these orientations shall be 'without prejudice' to the primary objective 'to maintain price stability'. Once again, therefore, it is the central bank which is in control, and the goal of price stability which dominates.

A second remarkable aspect of Article 105 concerns the definition of the stated objective: price stability. Some of the countries which have recently made their central banks independent have also adopted this objective, but in those not involved in the Maastricht process the government retains the right to instruct the central bank as to what is meant by price stability. The Maastricht Treaty confers no such rights on other bodies. Consequently, it is difficult to take the expression to mean anything other than what it says, which is that the ECB must pursue a zero rate of inflation, and indeed the ECB has said that it will aim to keep inflation in the range of 0–2 per cent. Some advocates present this as a great concession, but it is no such thing. Measured inflation is understood to overstate actual inflation by around about 1 per cent owing to the limitations of the way data are collected. Therefore, achieving a measured rate of 0–2 per cent means an actual rate of between plus and minus 1 per cent, or, on average, zero.

So the Treaty is perfectly clear, and leaves no room for doubt as to what is intended. Had it been, as some apologists are apt to say, the intention that the ECB target 'low inflation', or 'low inflation in normal circumstances', or some other more or less reasonable objective, it would have been easy to say so. But the Treaty says 'price stability'. And this, as will become apparent, is beyond any reasonable doubt, the road to economic disaster.

The Stability Pact

The Maastricht Treaty also restricts national fiscal policies. Article 104c 1 says simply, 'Member states shall avoid excessive deficits.' The fiscal deficit is the amount that a government borrows in a year, which is usually measured as a percentage of national income. More surprisingly, if member states fail to respect this requirement the European Union has the right, by Article 104c 11, 'to require the Member State concerned to make a non-interest-bearing deposit of an appropriate size with the Community until the excessive deficit has, in the view of the Council, been corrected' and 'to impose fines of an appropriate size'.

The details of the size of fines and circumstances in which they would be imposed were worked out in 1997. The rules are that, in principle, a country will be fined if it has a fiscal deficit of more than 3 per cent of national income unless its national income fell by 2 per cent or more in that year. Thus if there is a severe enough recession it will be excused the fine when it borrows too much. In other cases, whether the fine is actually imposed is subject to a vote, but first we should consider what the consequences of imposing the fines would be.

As a preliminary point, the concession that a 2 per cent fall in output means there will be no fine is not nearly as generous as it might seem. Such falls happen in something like two or three times every hundred years in the developed world.[19] Evidently, if the concession is to be meaningful, it must be that the authors of the Maastricht Treaty fear that their policy framework will result in many more severe recessions than there have been in the recent past.

Furthermore, one of the goals of government policy is to prevent sharp recessions. The idea that the Stability Pact comes within the bounds of reason because it permits proper policy on the condition that a huge economic failure has already occurred is astonishing. And in any case, the rules are relaxed only in the year when output makes this dramatic fall. The next year, let us hope it has stabilised. The need for government expenditure is the same since the recession is then no deeper, but nor has it gone. But the Pact rules are binding because output is not falling.[20]

One defence of the arrangements sometimes offered is to say that European countries now have healthier budgetary positions than they have had for some time – most are near enough in balance and some have a surplus. Therefore, it is said, from this starting position, the 3 per cent margin gives adequate room for manoeuvre. This is, however, not much good. In the first place, it is no kind of argument that the rule is a good one, merely a claim that the errors it embodies happen to be unimportant in present circumstances. In the second place, it would seem to assume that only the first few years of EMU are of any interest. After all, the 'starting position' cannot be expected to persist into the infinite future. But thirdly, recent history provides another of those facts so inconvenient for the euro-advocate, namely the deterioration of the British fiscal position during the ERM recession.

It will be recalled that late in the 1980s, Nigel Lawson achieved what was then the largest and most sustained fiscal surplus in post-war British history. One could hardly wish for a better starting position. Yet the ERM recession sent the government into a huge deficit, well over the 3 per cent level. On the standard British calculations, it was more like 8 per cent GDP, on the Maastricht definitions of what counts as a deficit, it reached about 6 per cent. It remained outside the Stability Pact limits well into the 1990s. Through this whole period, only in one year did output fall by 2 per cent, but only just.[21] So, the Stability Pact would have required the British government to make huge expenditure cuts (or tax increases) in the depths of recession. It should be remembered that unemployment reached 2.9 million even with the actual degree of government expenditure. How high would it have been if the government had been forced to improve its own balance by an amount equal to 3 per cent of national income? It is hard to say, but as must be apparent, that would have involved rather large tax increases, and a rather severe worsening of the recession.

The prospect is a terrible one, and the example is particularly haunting because so much of the recession was attributable to membership of the ERM. The advocates of the euro would like us to be locked into an exchange rate without the possibility of escape, and be subject to the fiscal rules as well.

It should also be said, of course, that if any Stability Pact fine were ever levied, it would be an extraordinary imposition on national sovereignty, without parallel anywhere in the world. The federal government of the United States, for example, does not impose rules on the budgetary policy of the states, and certainly not fines, although US states are usually thought to have rather less independence than EU member states. Some of the states have constitutional rules which bind them to balanced budgets, but this is a matter of an individual state's constitution, not a rule emanating from the federal government.

These rules alone make it clear that joining the euro raises significant issues of national sovereignty. It is not the purpose of this book to argue one way or the other on the issue of exactly what is meant by sovereignty or when and why it is important. But it should be noted that when advocates of the euro pretend that the only thing given up by joining EMU is the possibility of exchange-rate changes and of setting interest rates appropriately, and when they go on to deny that this could possibly raise any important constitutional issue, they are telling much less than the whole truth. Fiscal policy is also subject to tight restraint, and democratically elected national governments to fines.

Why does the Treaty say these things?

The natural-rate hypothesis

In 1968 Milton Friedman advanced the hypothesis that there exists a natural rate of unemployment. By this he meant, first, that left to itself the actual level of unemployment will remain around this rate, and, second, that the government cannot do anything with monetary or fiscal policy to keep the actual level of unemployment away from this level for long, although it might do harm in various ways if it tries. The basis of Friedman's argument was that labour markets work well in allowing people to sell their labour at the prevailing price if they wish to. If they do not wish to that is their business, but if they do, they will be able to. Unemployment, particularly long-term unemployment, is therefore more or less limited to people who do not wish to work.

It had been argued before Friedman, and was widely believed in the post-war period, that if the government were to undertake extra expenditure, financed by borrowing, this would increase the overall level of demand. The increase in demand would induce firms to hire more people, and this would reduce unemployment. Friedman's argument was that since this increase in demand does not originate in a change in individuals' preferences it lowers unemployment only by fooling them, and this can only be temporary. The government might, therefore, be able to engineer a temporary fall in unemployment, or a temporary rise, and booms and recessions might on occasion arise naturally. When in a boom, of course, unemployment would be below the natural rate, and when in a recession, above it, but these things would only be temporary.

In this view there are other factors which might affect unemployment on a long-term basis, but only by themselves being the determinants of the natural rate of unemployment. The most obvious of these is the level of unemployment benefits. If these are high enough more people will prefer to be unemployed, and therefore unemployment will be higher. Thus, argue the followers of Friedman, if a government wishes to reduce unemployment, lowering benefits and other similar measures will do some good. But as far as monetary policy and the overall level of government expenditure and taxation are concerned there can be no long-term effect on employment, either beneficial or harmful. Unemployment reverts to the natural rate.

Whether Friedman's argument for the existence of a natural rate of unemployment should really be considered part of the monetarist doctrine is a moot point, but it is not relevant. What is important is one inference that is routinely drawn from Friedman's argument: that monetary policymakers should give all their attention to the control of inflation and none to the control of unemployment. This is the idea that most clearly motivates the Maastricht Treaty.

There is no denying that Friedman's argument is a powerful one. But powerful or not, I shall argue that it is demonstrably false and that a disregard for employment in setting monetary and fiscal policy does great damage. First, however, we must note a further turn of the screw added to Friedman's hypothesis by later theorists, and the prevalence in modern thinking of the doctrine of policy credibility.

Two arguments for central bank independence

There is a peculiar aspect to the way the case for central bank independence has been made. Two quite different arguments have been advanced, in most cases without any clear distinction being drawn between them, even though they depend on more or less contradictory assumptions. As it happens both the arguments are incorrect, but this does not stop them having a powerful influence on European policymaking.

The doctrine of policy credibility

The doctrine of policy credibility holds that an important determinant of economic success is the belief of businesses and individuals that the policymaker will maintain low inflation. The emphasis rests firmly on belief in this argument. What the policymaker actually does is of secondary importance.

A typical formulation of the doctrine would be that if wage bargainers expect high inflation they will set high wage increases. This in itself more or less forces the policymaker to deliver high inflation; otherwise many workers will be priced out of their jobs by the high wages. The resultant unemployment would be temporary, of course, according to Friedman's argument, but painful nonetheless. If the wage bargainers could be made to believe that there was going to be low inflation, they would agree lower wages and thereby make the low inflation possible. However, it is also said that once low wage increases have been agreed, the policymaker can achieve a temporary fall in unemployment by actually delivering high inflation. This awkward consideration is supposed to make it difficult to convince the wage bargainers, who are assumed to have a detailed understanding of the objectives of the policymaker, that inflation will be low, thereby leaving us permanently stuck with high wage increases and so, presumably, high inflation.

Sometimes the credibility argument is reformulated to say that it is not really the expectations of wage bargainers which are important, but rather those of financial markets. These markets, it is claimed, are permanently sceptical of governments because bursts of inflation have the effect of reducing the real value of government debt. Therefore a government wishing to reduce its debt without paying it back has an incentive to attempt to spring a surprise inflation on the markets since this erodes the real value of the government's debt. This, it is said, means the markets always demand higher interest than they would in the absence of this threat. The simple solution to this is for the government to issue index-linked debt. Lenders will then have no reason to concern themselves with forecasting inflation: whatever it turns out to be, they will be appropriately compensated.

The fashionable solution to the wage-setting problem is to assume that an independent central bank can undertake to deliver low inflation and the wage bargainers will believe this, whereupon the problem is solved. This idea makes it clear why the commitment of the Maastricht

Treaty to price stability should be so uncompromising. Although it seems extreme, it is in fact rationalised by the doctrine of credibility.

Thus it is argued that central bank independence is a free lunch, in that it lowers expected inflation without any offsetting detriment. One or two charts purporting to support this view have been popularised by *The Economist* magazine, among others, in arguing for independence of the Bank of England. There are many problems with this evidence, but perhaps the most serious is that the analysis on which it was based has now been shown to be factually incorrect.[22]

'Politicians cannot be trusted'

Although the doctrine of credibility is fashionable among academic supporters of the euro, the more popular argument for central bank independence among both policymakers and commentators is that voters are myopic so that policy can be adjusted to secure short-term benefits before elections, even if this does long-term damage. Politicians, who are generally in the business of seeking re-election, are, in this argument, likely to lower interest rates before an election to reduce unemployment even if it means inflation rises after the election. The result is bad policy. In this case, the benefit of central bank independence is that the bankers have no electoral incentives and so policy is better.

Clearly, this argument depends on voters being short-sighted. If they properly understand what the government is doing, they will not be impressed and will presumably vote it out. This is rather in contrast to the assumption made in the first argument about the sophisticated insight into policy supposedly possessed by wage bargainers. Confusion is further heightened by the fact that the second argument is sometimes said to show that central bank independence improves credibility, even though that notion has no place in the account.

The idea of excessive deficits

In parallel to the theory of monetary policy which motivated the Maastricht Treaty, another theory claimed that fiscal policy can do no good either, but can do harm. It can do no good, it was said, because when governments borrow money they deprive some private agent of the funds, and thereby prevent a beneficial investment project being undertaken. It can do harm, it is claimed, in one of two ways.

The first argument is that when one country in a monetary union borrows, this has the effect of raising the interest rate that other borrowers must pay, including other governments. If this really made an argument for regulation of borrowing it would have wide-ranging implications, since the same point could be made about any agent's purchase of any commodity. If one government purchases 'too many' paper clips no doubt their price will rise, but it would be bizarre to find international penalties being imposed for such a 'transgression'.

A different argument, which is given much more prominence by the European Commission, is that if a government borrows too much it may eventually find itself unable to repay its loans. In such a circumstance, it is unlikely that a developed-world government would formally repudiate its debt, since this would have so many serious ramifications throughout the financial sector. In order to prevent this, however, a rescue might have to be organised by other countries. In the case of the European Union it is reasonable to suppose that much of the burden of such a rescue would fall on other members. The repayment of one country's debt would then fall ultimately on the taxpayers of other countries. This is what led Emerson *et al.* to claim that 'Fiscal discipline defined as the avoidance of an unsustainable build-up of public debt is therefore a vital condition' for the success of EMU.'[23]

There is no doubt, of course, that a default would be a serious matter. It is not clear why the fear of one should have become so prominent in the Maastricht process, since there would have been much the same consequences of default at an earlier stage. Be that as it may, the important issue is whether the danger of default is sufficient for it to be a major policy concern for the European Union as a whole, and, if so, what measures are likely to generate good, sustainable fiscal policy.

The errors in the Treaty

There is no such thing as a natural rate of unemployment

There is no doubt that Friedman's idea of a natural rate of unemployment has great appeal, and for many economists it has become the basic rule of thumb in thinking about unemployment. However, we should not allow theory to blind us to the facts, or be unduly impressed by the notoriously changeable fashions of economists.

There are two alternatives to the natural-rate view. One is the view that Friedman was specifically attacking: that unemployment can be permanently lowered by a policy of permanently higher inflation and that a government can in principle achieve any desired unemployment rate if it is prepared to put up with the corresponding level of inflation. This is sometimes known as the Phillips-curve view. Friedman's attack on this was certainly effective. But the trap lies in thinking that because the view Friedman attacked was wrong, his own must be right.

There is an alternative to Friedman's view which is much more important than the Phillips-curve view. This is the idea that the rate of unemployment which is currently achievable depends on the recent history of unemployment. So, for example, one consequence of a long and deep recession, which temporarily raises unemployment above any estimate of its natural rate, is that for a long period thereafter it will be all but impossible to return unemployment to the levels previously attainable. This will be true whatever the level of inflation.

This idea, sometimes known as the 'hysteresis' view, is illustrated clearly by the British experience, shown in Figure 3.1. Between 1945 and 1979 the highest level of unemployment reached was 6 per cent in 1977. At the time, such a level was thought to be a disaster. The Conservative government elected in 1979 advocated the natural-rate view, asserting that monetary policy could permanently change only the rate of inflation and that it could not affect unemployment beyond the short run. During the recession that followed unemployment increased well beyond 6 per cent. It was claimed, however, that this would be temporary, and that once inflation had fallen, unemployment would return to its natural rate.

Figure 3.1 **British unemployment, 1975–96**

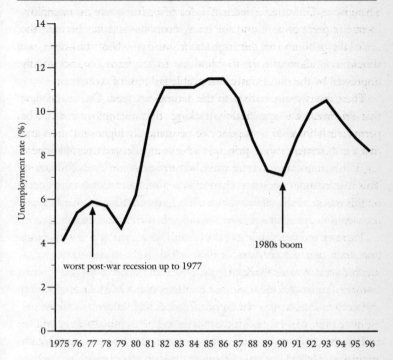

Source: OECD.

The sequel is now notorious. Unemployment did fall, but it was allowed to fall 'too far', so that inflation once again became a problem. A boom developed rapidly at the end of the 1980s and a further recession followed as the government once again tried to reduce inflation. Much argument has naturally taken place as to why the boom was allowed to go so far without corrective action and how the subsequent recession could have been ended. Much less often discussed is what happened to unemployment in this period. The lowest level that unemployment reached was 7 per cent; that is, 1 per cent higher than its level at the previous worst in the post-war period.

Since 1977 was a recession year, by Friedman's account unemployment (at 6 per cent) must have been above the natural rate; and since 1990 was a boom year, unemployment (at 7 per cent) must have been below it. Furthermore, 1977 was at that time the worst recession in the post-war period, and the boom of 1990 became notorious for its extravagance, so in each case the deviations from the natural rate should have been large. Clearly, the data contradict the view that there is any such thing as a natural rate of unemployment and show that long and deep recessions can have long-term effects on employment.

The natural-rate theorists have a response to this, which is to say that the natural rate may change depending on the incentives and organisation of the labour market. This gives rise to so-called supply-side policies aimed at lowering the natural rate. Policies usually claimed to improve the functioning of the labour market include lowering benefits and reducing tax rates, both of which are intended to encourage people to seek work. Reducing the power of trade unions and limiting workers' rights are also commonly mentioned. Other policies said to improve incentives might also be included, such as privatisations.

However, when we compare Britain in 1990 with Britain in 1977, it is clear that the supply-side conditions can only have improved. Marginal tax rates and the real value of benefits were cut, and union powers and workers' rights were reduced. Extensive privatisation was undertaken. Yet, after the long, deep recession of the early 1980s, or slightly later in most of continental Europe, unemployment failed to return to the levels which were previously thought disasters, let alone to those which were normal. Therefore, whatever good the supply-side reforms did, it was not adequate to counteract the harm done by the disregard for unemployment as an objective of monetary policy during the period. This disregard led to a recession which did great and long-lasting damage in the form of a persistently higher level of unemployment.

Nor is the British case exceptional. Among European countries the

Figure 3.2   **French unemployment, 1975–96**

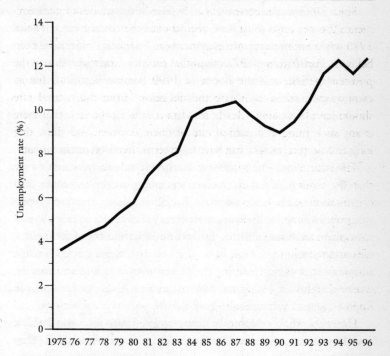

Source: OECD.

British experience, as regards unemployment, has been rather better than most. The case of France, shown in Figure 3.2, is remarkable. Unemployment there has rose in seventeen of the twenty-two years from 1975 to 1996. Although it has fallen more recently, we can only marvel at policymakers who insist that there is a natural rate of unemployment to which the actual unemployment level invariably returns, with reasonable speed and of its own accord. Similar data could be presented for most countries of the European Union.

No doubt someone will try to argue that my ending of the data in 1996 is unfair. Not at all – it is no secret that unemployment has fallen in most countries since then, the members of the euro area included. But the lessons of a long period show that the natural rate view of unemployment is wrong. No one has ever said that it is impossible for the euro area to enjoy good times – of course unemployment will sometimes fall there. But it is very foolish to base one's policy on what one remembers from the last couple of years. History can only teach the lessons we are willing to learn, and it is the historical record on which my argument is based.

It is true that in some countries, such as the United States, one could believe there is some support for the natural-rate hypothesis. But these countries have not experienced the long and deep recessions that Britain and France have. So the US case is equally consistent with either the natural-rate view or the hysteresis view. Since so many European experiences resemble the British and French in contradicting the natural-rate view, we are forced to conclude that, elegant as Friedman's argument is, it is not correct. The labour market is a more complex market than his view suggests, and we cannot rely on quickly reaching a point where all who wish to work are able to.

The important consideration is that long and deep recessions, which leave large numbers of people unemployed, raise the minimum level of unemployment achievable for a long time thereafter. It is difficult to be precise about the reasons for this, although there are many possibilities. One is that many people unemployed for long periods of time lose their skills or motivation, or may appear to have done so, and are therefore less attractive to potential employers. Firms which are liquidated during the recession do not automatically come back into existence when the recession ends, so there is a permanent loss of the capital they scrap and of the firm-specific expertise of their former employees. Also, if recession is associated with an overvaluation of the currency, as has generally been the case in Britain, export markets are lost and not necessarily regained when the exchange rate falls again.

THE ARGUMENTS AGAINST THE EURO

The consequence is that economic policy must not be set in accordance with the design of the Maastricht Treaty. Inflation is not welcome, but it does not follow that under all circumstances the achievement of price stability should be the exclusive goal of policy. Circumstances have arisen, and will arise again, where some mild degree of inflation is a far lesser evil than the long-term damage done by a deep recession which may be needed to eliminate all trace of it.

A good example of such circumstances is again to be found in German unification. German policy was clearly unsuitable for the other EU member states, and under the ERM they followed it to their cost. But there is another issue: was it even good policy for Germany? Unification brought many problems. Once it became possible for east Germans to buy western products they did so in fairly large numbers, and this led to a degree of inflation pressure. At the same time, once it became possible for east Germans to migrate to west Germany, they could not be expected to work in the east for substantially lower wages than were available in the west, so eastern wages rose. This, combined with economic collapse in the rest of eastern Europe and the former Soviet Union, did great damage to the profitability of east German firms, many of which went bankrupt, creating unemployment in the east. The German government decided against substantial tax increases to finance social security, investment subsidies and other payments that it was making to the east. It was forced to borrow the required amount instead, so there was a deterioration of German public finances.

Of all these problems, the Bundesbank decided that inflation was the one that should be tackled. It therefore increased interest rates. The consequences were a slowdown of economic activity, which increased unemployment in both east and west; an appreciation of the Deutschmark, which was particularly pernicious for the east German firms on the margin of viability; and, as a result of the deterioration in economic performance, a further deterioration of government finances. More than ten years later the adverse consequences are still apparent. Unemployment remains at excessive levels, and Germany came within a whisker of failing the Maastricht fiscal criteria for EMU membership.

Although the best policy response to unification would have involved tax increases in the west, this was not within the power of the Bundesbank. It had to determine what interest rate to set, and there was an alternative to what it did: to accept a degree of inflation. Meanwhile, attention could have been given to the lack of competitiveness of east German firms and every effort made to keep in business those which might be viable by, most importantly, resisting a rise in the value of the Deutschmark, indeed, by seeking to lower it if possible.

This would have resulted in higher prices. It would also have moderated the rise in unemployment and the deterioration of public finances. It is a matter of judgement which is the more serious. But it is easy to see that the public debt which Germany has needlessly acquired brings a permanent cost; and unemployment has certainly not proved a temporary problem. German inflation, as it turned out, never rose much above 5 per cent, hardly a level that would have been a catastrophe even if it had been somewhat higher.[24]

Advocates of the euro like to argue that the reform of the east German economy would inevitably impose serious costs, so that the experience of the German economy since unification is wholly unrepresentative of anything which is to be expected in the future, but they should not be allowed to. The sustained increase in unemployment that Germany has experienced contradicts the natural-rate hypothesis on which the Bundesbank based, and the ECB bases, policy, but there is nothing exceptional in this. The British and French experiences, as well as those of many other countries, also contradict it. It is true that taxes should have been raised in west Germany, but this does not excuse further bad policy by the central bank. In any case, the commitment not to raise taxes was made in the context of forecasts about the consequences of unification, which were much more optimistic. They said, in effect, that a great investment opportunity had arisen in east Germany, and that this would accelerate growth and therefore brought no need for increased taxes. These forecasts were based on the same assumptions as the natural-rate hypothesis, and they also turned out to be badly wrong.

So the view that the control of inflation should always be the over-riding priority has been tested in Germany, and it has been shown to lead to bad policy. Germany, as well as the rest of Europe, would have been better served by a policy that sought to balance economic objectives, not to prioritise one and only one above the rest. The German economy may have been successful for decades, but the policy of the Bundesbank, which is the policy of the Maastricht Treaty, has changed that.

The danger of the Maastricht Treaty, then, lies in disregarding unemployment and other objectives when seeking to control inflation. This certainly does not mean that inflation is beneficial, but it does mean that its elimination should not always be the sole objective. In particular, faced with inflationary developments over which policy-makers have no control, it should not generally be their priority to eliminate it immediately. In contrast, the Maastricht Treaty's insistence that the ECB achieve price stability seems to give no scope for anything else, whatever the cost in unemployment. This will be a tragedy, since it was the attitude in Britain in 1981, or Germany in 1990, or France for most of the 1980s and 1990s, and we already know that the costs are severe and long term.

Credibility is of no significance
The academic version of the credibility argument
Perhaps the most important challenge to the idea that credibility is all important in affecting the wage-bargaining process is that it is difficult to find instances of people bargaining their wages on the basis of what they think inflation will be in the future. Many people no doubt start off by thinking what wage increase is required to compensate for past inflation; a few perhaps project past inflation forward as a rough guide to what future inflation may be. But what the theory requires is that

people form an acute sense of what the policymakers' incentives are under a variety of circumstances, and base their wage bargain on an assessment of how future policy will affect inflation. As a description of the world, this is plainly fantastic.

Second, there is the awkward point that all central banks now seem to think that policy takes two years to affect inflation, and the vast majority of wage bargains are for a shorter period. This means that at the time the wage bargain is struck, policymakers have no control over inflation for the period of the bargain. Therefore no issues arise about what the policymaker says future policy will be. What is happening is that policymakers take their decisions and then wage bargainers bargain their wages. If it is important to them what policymakers have done, they can find out. No issue about believing or disbelieving what they say arises.[25]

The argument that politicians cannot be trusted

This argument, although again fashionable, does not stand up to much scrutiny. The argument is that politicians are persistently tempted to adopt inflationary policy in order to win elections. But does inflationary policy win elections? If it is necessary to indulge in simple-minded explanations of electoral outcomes, a rather better picture comes from thinking of governments as being rewarded for doing what they say they will do.

The Heath government, in 1970, promised a free market and sound finance. It delivered nationalisation and inflation, losing power in 1974. Labour, elected in high hopes of peaceful relations with the trade union movement, was never more damaged than by the 'winter of discontent' in 1978–9. Margaret Thatcher, however, is a clear case of a politician who did what she said she would do, although it was unpleasant, and was rewarded with election victory in 1983 despite unemployment rising towards 3 million. John Major survived the election of 1992 in most unpleasant economic circumstances promising commitment to the EMS; after the devaluation later that year his opinion-poll rating never recovered, and the government was defeated, although economic performance had been improving substantially ever since the devaluation.

The boom of the late 1980s appears to many people to offer a strong case for the political-manipulation view of economic management. Even if there were nothing to the contrary to be said, one example hardly establishes a general tendency. In fact, there is reason to believe that this boom was a genuine mistake. The lack of substantial independent commentary to the effect that policy was misdirected before the 1987 election, the failure to reverse policy after it, indeed the continuation of expansionary measures, and the fact that, fast though the economy was growing, this was broadly the outcome that had been promised as the reward for the policies of the early 1980s all point to its being a mistake.

It has also been widely, though groundlessly, asserted that the public disputes between the then Chancellor of the Exchequer, Kenneth Clarke, and the governor of the Bank of England, Eddie George, before the 1997 election demonstrate the case for independence. At that time interest rates were controlled by the chancellor. The governor persistently advocated an increase on the basis that he felt that in two years' time inflation would be too high. The chancellor made a different judgement and refused the increase, earning plenty of criticism from the financial press for political manipulation and such like. Yet the verdict of history is that Clarke was right. If the quality of monetary policy is to be judged by the inflation rate it delivers, Kenneth Clarke's decisions have been entirely vindicated. An interest-rate increase in early 1997 would have been wrong and damaging. We were lucky not to have an independent central bank at that time and on these terms there is no case to answer that there was a political manipulation taking place.

Lastly, as regards the most important points of economics, there is the issue of whether interest-rate changes are a sensible way for politicians to try to buy votes anyway. Many savers are hurt by interest-rate cuts, and this factor must counteract the borrowers who benefit. There is also the point that tax cuts offer an alternative to interest-rate cuts. Most voters pay tax, so most votes would, on the assumptions being made, be for sale. So, if the problem is that elected people, rather than doing broadly what they perceive to be in the national interest, are merely in the business of buying votes, it makes no sense to focus on central bank independence as the remedy.

Probably more important than the logical deficiencies of this argument is the attitude we are invited to take to democratic accountability. It is an assumption of the Maastricht approach that unelected, unremovable and unaccountable individuals will pursue the general interest. Personally, I am much happier with the view that people who fail, or are incompetent, or who pursue sectional or personal interests, or who lie, can be fired. These are among the fruits of democracy. That the opposite view is now becoming engrained in the thinking of the European Union, and that the elected representatives of the people are dismissed as 'gerrymandering' is one of the most frightening aspects of what is becoming the culture of the integrationist.

Balancing the government budget can be damaging
What is good fiscal policy?

There is no doubt that a default by a government would be a serious matter. Equally, there should be no doubt that there is much more to sound fiscal policy than the reduction of deficits; and, indeed, even the avoidance of default, or the danger of it, may not be an entirely simple matter of reducing government spending or increasing taxes. The Maastricht rules certainly have the effect of preventing the proper use of fiscal policy, and the countries that have been seeking to follow them have not achieved satisfactory fiscal positions either.

The truth about fiscal policy is that governments of developed countries routinely run deficits. No serious problem need arise, as it would for a household, because developed economies continually grow, so that the government's tax base is always increasing. It is surprising at first sight, but nevertheless quite clear, that a government can borrow every year and still have a stable or even falling burden of debt relative to national income. British government debt today, even if calculated at constant prices, is far in excess of what would have been sustainable in the nineteenth century. But so what? British national income is far higher too, and so the debt can be sustained.

Beyond this, a proper understanding of fiscal policy needs to see government borrowing in the context of the behaviour of the private sector and the activity of the economy as a whole. The crucial point is that economic transactions are two-sided. If the government spends less money, someone receives less. If instead of spending less the government taxes more, it is much the same: someone else has less. Whoever has less will also presumably spend less, which is the same thing as another person receiving less. All the people receiving less will then pay less in tax, so the government's revenues will fall. Consequently, the government's borrowing will not fall by as much as its spending since the cut in spending itself causes a fall in tax receipts. This means that the achievement of a balanced budget, or a nearly balanced budget, is much more complex than it seems. It is emphatically not a matter merely of hard decisions on spending cuts or tax increases, and the presumption that it is neglects the economic effects of these actions.

It is sometimes argued that a government which is trying to balance its budget can cut expenditure and counteract the tendency of this to lower employment by reducing interest rates. This is supposed to encourage the private sector to invest more, thereby generating jobs and hence tax revenue. But in the context of central bank independence, and certainly monetary union, the interest rate is controlled by someone else. We are more likely to find ourselves in the position of having monetary policy causing unemployment and fiscal policy being prevented, by the Maastricht rules, from acting as an antidote. In any case it is far from clear that interest-rate reductions automatically call forth extra investment of just the required amount.

It is true, of course, that overall saving and investment will be equal, but it is a mistake to think that saving by the government therefore automatically increases investment by the private sector. When the government saves more (or borrows less), the private sector as a whole suffers a fall in its income because it is receiving less money from the government, whether in benefits or payments for goods and services. This fall should be expected primarily to cause private-sector saving to decrease, not investment to increase. The reasons are that at a lower level of income the private sector has less money to save, and, at the same time, investment projects will, if anything, be less attractive because the private sector also has less money to spend. So sure enough, saving and investment are equal, even after the government saves more, but it is because income has fallen enough to decrease private saving rather than because investment has spontaneously increased in response to government cuts. The odd 0.25 per cent cut in interest rates is unlikely to counteract this, and in adverse conditions there may be no interest rate low enough to call forth sufficient extra investment to maintain employment in the face of government expenditure cuts. In Japan, for example, interest rates have been cut more or less to zero without ever having the desired effect on investment.

If conditions become bad enough, private agents may think it in their interests to save more as a precautionary move. Any extra saving is just like the government reducing its borrowing in implying a fall in others' income. It will make investment projects less attractive too.

Therefore the view that balancing the government budget, or moving from a larger to a smaller deficit, necessarily improves overall economic performance depends on one of two mistakes. Either it is being forgotten that an action by the government which reduces its expenditure or raises its income necessarily also reduces the income of the private sector as a whole, or it is being assumed that private-sector investment depends only on the interest rate and not at all on the general degree of economic health, and in particular private-sector spending power, and that some unspecified, but convenient, force causes just the right degree of investment to be called forth by any government tax or expenditure change.

A good demonstration of the problems of fiscal management again comes from recent European experience. Once the European recession after German unification began to be felt, causing government revenue to fall and expenditure to rise, several governments began to fear that they would fail to meet the convergence rules, and in particular that their fiscal deficits would be above 3 per cent of national income. The case of France is illustrative. In 1993 its fiscal deficit was 4.5 per cent.[26] The OECD reported that 'the 1994 budget aimed at unprecedented expenditure restriction'. The next year, after this restriction, the French deficit was 4.8 per cent of national income. In its 1995 annual report on France the OECD reported that 'the 1995 budget … aimed at expenditure restraint and a further fall in the deficit'. This time the outcome was a deficit of 4.3 per cent of national income. In 1997 the OECD reported 'the 1996 budget was again aimed at expenditure restraint and a further decrease in the deficit', and in 1996 the deficit was 3.9 per cent of national income. Thus unprecedented restraint followed by years of further contraction had only a marginal impact on the overall budgetary position. In the end, as is well known, France and several other countries were only able to achieve a deficit of below 3 per cent by what became known as 'fiscal fudges', meaning creative accounting. All their determined economic policy, which imposed so much hardship through expenditure cuts and so much long-term damage through government investment cuts, failed to bring the forecast results.

It is important to be clear that this sequence of policy decisions was motivated by the same theoretical outlook as is now encapsulated in the Stability Pact. Although these events took place before 1999, the convergence criteria to which governments were trying to conform are similar to the Stability Pact rules. Nor can it be pretended that this failure is explained by German unification. That took place in 1990. It cannot explain the failure of expenditure cutting to bring a significant fall in the French government's deficit five years later. Although it would be convenient to advocates of the Maastricht plan to argue it, there should also be no question that the failure of policy was owing to a lack of will on the part of the government. The OECD reports make it quite clear that the hard choices were being made. The problem was that the economic theory on which the policy was based is inadequate. What happened was that French expenditure cuts damaged the French economy, and that prevented the government's finances improving.

So what should we do? It is no easy matter to construct appropriate rules for fiscal policy. This fact itself speaks against the simple rules of the Maastricht programme. However, it is certainly asking too much of governments to offset every change in private-sector behaviour. For this reason alone economic fluctuations are inevitable.

The danger of the Stability Pact is that it prevents the exercise of sensible judgement and pushes in the direction of counterproductive policy. Faced with an economic downturn, a government finds its finances worsening. If it is in danger of breaching Pact limits, it must start to raise taxes and cut expenditure, both of which worsen the downturn. If the downturn becomes critical the fiscal rules are relaxed, but by then the damage has been done.

Can we hope that the fines will not be imposed? Yes, this is always a possibility. However, there are two serious reasons to doubt that this will be an effective remedy. First, the doctrine of credibility argues that rules must be strictly imposed. What will the financial markets think if the first time the Pact is breached, political leaders of the European Union club together and vote not to impose a fine? This consideration alone suggests that the fine will be imposed in order to preserve the EU's 'credibility'.

Second, even in the absence of a fine, we should still expect countries to be shy of breaching the agreed limits and then having to be dispensed from the fine. Since, furthermore, fiscal control is far from being an exact science, governments will presumably wish to be well clear of the limits. This consideration points towards a permanent and general attempt at fiscal contraction to provide security against either being fined, or being embarrassed by being let off the fine.

This creates a significant danger of generally contractionary policy. It is all very well to suppose that governments will have to aim at something like a balanced budget in order to be safe from the fine. But this is not good policy. First, there is no powerful reason to seek a balanced budget on its own merits. Developed-country incomes grow and therefore a growing public debt associated with a normally unbalanced budget can be sustainable. Second, it is not clear that the achievement of a balanced budget on average over a long period will be reasonably practicable. The French, and others, found it difficult if not impossible to achieve a deficit of under 3 per cent in time for the euro in 1999, despite having seven years to achieve it since they signed the Treaty. Why should it be so easy to achieve a balance any time it is desired without causing unemployment? Again, it is easy for the euro-enthusiast to point to a temporary circumstance of near balance around Europe and wish the problem away, but we are not discussing whether a balanced budget is possible or desirable today. We are discussing policymaking institutions for the long-term future.

What we need is not a collection of rules and international fines on governments that borrow too much, but a recognition that the government's borrowing is to a large extent determined by the decisions of the private sector, and therefore that healthy public finances are to an important degree the outcome of a healthy economy. Imposing 'discipline' on public finances is much more likely to worsen private-sector confidence and lower investment than it is to promote the investment which, if it occurred, would automatically result in an improvement of the public finances. Treating the symptoms, in this case, makes the disease worse. We should be looking at what makes an economy healthy and expecting the achievement of this to improve public finances, rather than expecting cutting government expenditure somehow to improve the health of the economy.

It is worth noting that in opposite circumstances even balancing the government budget may not be sufficient. If private-sector spending is sufficiently high the government should be in surplus. In this case, even a balanced budget leads to excessive demand. It is easy to imagine a government spending too much in a boom through being unduly impressed that its budget was balanced. The signs, on the basis of the theory behind Maastricht, would be that the government was doing a good job, exercising prudence and promoting stability by balancing its budget. But there is no reason to suppose that good management should not require a considerable surplus. This consideration lies behind the idea that the government budget should balance over the trade cycle, meaning that it will be in surplus during booms and in deficit during recessions. This is all very well, but there is no automatic mechanism to ensure that the degree of surplus or deficit will be the right one. In any case, neither the Maastricht rules nor the Stability Pact places limits on budgetary positions over the trade cycle. They simply place limits on deficits.

The problem of international co-ordination

A further ramification arises from the international effects of budgetary policy. If small countries have a strict balanced-budget policy it may not hurt them. Fluctuations in demand at home can be offset by changes in exports, roughly maintaining employment. Thus the fact that Luxembourg and Switzerland have had long histories of economic success but have rarely borrowed more than tiny amounts is no surprise. Even Germany in the period of its greatest success borrowed little and exported much, but the significance of Germany in the world economy was much less then than now. No doubt this also explains why so many US states choose to have balanced-budget policies. Each state is small, so individually their budgets are of little significance.

However, a large economy, say the whole of the European Union, cannot expect to escape in this way. A fall in demand in the EU is not likely to be offset by an increase in exports, since such an increase would have to be huge relative to the rest of the world's total imports. Indeed, the problem will be made worse if a recession in Europe also reduces imports from the rest of the world, as presumably it must. This will push the rest of the world's economies in the direction of recession as well, reducing European exports to them.

In such a case, it would need to be accepted that the world as a whole can have a high level of employment only if the things supplied by employed people are purchased by someone. In part this will mean they must be purchased by Europeans. If private-sector demand is high enough, then that is all well and good. But when it is not, there is a need for governments to act. In certain cases, this will require governments to do far more than observe the naïve view of 'prudence' which dominates the Maastricht Treaty. It will be necessary to set policy, not according to the rules, but according to the conditions.

What the world as a whole desperately needs, then, is a European policy which acknowledges the international interdependence of economies. The idea that Europeans should look after their own problems and leave the rest of the world to sort themselves out, is a denial of this basic fact. Yet the notion that other countries should put their own houses in order simply makes no sense when it is recognised that economic transactions are two-sided. We cannot have a policy of Asia exporting more without a policy of someone else importing more and for this to happen, without an increase in unemployment, someone must spend more.

The fiscal consequences of Maastricht

Although any country can find itself in difficulty because of excessive government budget cutting, three considerations make the problem worse in the Maastricht case. First, the rules are incorporated in an international agreement and are therefore much harder to change than the rules of thumb governments adopt for their own purposes. The details of the rules are not part of the Treaty itself so they are easier to change than the central bank statutes. But they are still embedded in international agreement.

Second, they are associated with fines. With a proper understanding of fiscal policy these are a strikingly bad idea. The fines would have to be levied on just those governments in no position to pay them. We are to contemplate the case of a government which has been unable to cut its deficit, although it will presumably have made some effort to do so, thereby bringing about a recession. It is then required to raise taxes to pay the fine. The authors of this proposal seem to think that excessive borrowing by a government is analogous to a road-traffic offence and that a firm enough punishment will deter future infringements. But we are dealing with governments whose every financial action affects the balance of the economy. In the case envisaged, the extra 'discipline' or 'commitment' expected of the 'delinquent' government can lead only to action which further reduces private-sector incomes and hence worsens recession. It is incomprehensible that anyone could imagine this to be the way to build a successful political union.

Third, the fiscal rules are being imposed just when the ECB's monetary policy will be coming into effect. The monetary policy is in danger of creating recessionary circumstances all too often, but it is absolutely inevitable that it will do so somewhere at some time. In these circumstances rendering fiscal policy impotent as well creates a serious problem and then makes it unsolvable.

Might defaults happen?

The Maastricht rules are foolish rules because they force governments into counterproductive policy. But this does not mean that a government default would not be a serious matter. The fact that as long as governments conduct normally prudent policy there should be no danger of a default does not, unfortunately, mean that when policy is set in accordance with the Maastricht presumptions, such a danger can be ruled out. Table 3.1 shows the change in the ratio of government debt to national income between 1991 and 1996, expressed as a percentage.

Out of fifteen countries, all of which broadly adopted the Maastricht outlook on policy priorities and most of which were committed to meeting fiscal rules to qualify for monetary union, only one, Ireland,

Table 3.1 **Ratio of government debt to national income in EU member states, 1991 and 1996 (%)**

	1991	1996
Austria	58.1	69.5
Belgium	127.7	126.9
Denmark	62.3	66.7
Finland	23.0	58.0
France	35.8	55.4
Germany	41.5	60.4
Greece	92.3	112.6
Ireland	95.3	72.7
Italy	101.5	123.8
Luxembourg	4.2	6.6
Netherlands	78.8	76.6
Portugal	68.7	68.1
Spain	45.8	70.6
Sweden	53.0	77.4
United Kingdom	35.5	54.2

Source: OECD (1998).

the beneficiary of a high level of foreign investment, managed a significant reduction in its debt ratio, and three managed small improvements. The performance of France and Germany, the two leaders of the process and principal authors of the Treaty, is truly spectacular. In 1991 a Treaty was signed which was to exclude from EMU any country with a debt ratio greater than 60 per cent. No doubt France and Germany, starting from ratios of 36 per cent and 42 per cent, felt they had written a Treaty that made their own membership safe. Yet within five years there was a serious question as to whether they would be able to meet the criterion. Once again it should be emphasised that these have not been years of profligacy by European governments; they are not years of vote-buying politicians ruining the public finance to secure re-election. No, they are years of the Maastricht policy in action; years of central bank independence, sound money and 'prudence'. They are years of the things that we are promised in a monetary union will secure our well-being. Had the Maastricht rules been more tightly interpreted, countries with debt ratios well over 60 per cent would have been excluded. This proved to be too much of a political embarrassment, so the rule was for practical purposes ignored. Again, it is no secret that things have improved since 1996 – and improved by a surprising amount in some cases. But, as with the case of unemployment, the key lesson to draw – the one the euro-advocates would much rather ignore or brush away – is about the consequences of the Maastricht policy. The commitment in 1991 – the year of the Treaty – was to reduce government indebtedness by 'commitment' and 'firmness'. That commitment and firmness was indeed applied, but being based on bad economics, it did not bring the desired result. That is a lesson we should learn. Since then, there has been a world economic boom led by the United States, European economies have grown, this has made it much easier for governments to reduce borrowing, and the fiscal positions have improved. No one denies these things. But the Stability Pact is not a device anyone advocates because it is harmless in good times – to advocate it, one must believe it is helpful in bad times. And if we look at the record of bad times, this recent period tells a clear story.

Could bad times return, and what would happen if they did? Clearly they could. Indeed the interest rate cuts by the Federal Reserve at the beginning of 2001 are motivated precisely by the fear that they are returning. If recession begins in the United States and Japan, and arrives in Europe, does the Stability Pact equip us to deal with it? If growth slows or stops, if recession returns, euro area governments will find that, if they are to stay within the Stability Pact, they have little room for manoeuvre, and it will take only a slight reversal of fortune before they are again obliged to make expenditure cuts or tax increases.

If the lesson of the early 1990s were learned, the Stability Pact would be scrapped. The efforts of the euro advocates to distract attention from this real lesson of history, by protesting that things have improved since, reveals, sadly, that the lessons have not been learned.[27]

4 Is Britain special?

It is frequently argued that the British economy is different from those of continental Europe in a fairly permanent way and that this changes the balance of advantages and disadvantages of the euro.

One argument is that British trade patterns have traditionally been less European in their orientation than those of other countries. Consequently, we have less to gain from the removal of transactions costs and exchange-rate uncertainty within Europe and more to lose from any increased exchange-rate uncertainty with respect to the rest of the world.

The second argument is that more people in Britain have variable-rate mortgages than in most of Europe. British consumers are therefore more sensitive to interest-rate changes than those of, say, Germany. Therefore a European Central Bank (ECB) seeking, unavoidably, to employ a one-size-fits-all interest-rate policy to manage the whole European economy will, other things being equal, impose much more violent swings on Britain than elsewhere. It is also true, although the point is less frequently made, that British companies have rather more variable-rate loans than their continental counterparts. Again, therefore, we are better off preserving our own interest-rate policy.

The idea advanced by Christopher Huhne – that the higher proportion of flexible-rate loans is offset by a higher proportion of flexible-rate assets – is only half right. This characteristic does go some way to limit the difference between Britain and other countries in their overall responsiveness to interest-rate changes, but there is still the issue of the severity of effect on individuals. In the event of steeply rising interest rates, for example, many British households could find themselves unable to pay their mortgages. The fact that other British people would at the same time be benefiting, which is the extent of the point, would not be much consolation. In a case where this situation is extreme enough to lead to large numbers of defaults in Britain, the solvency of British financial services firms would be in danger, not those of other European countries.

The third frequently heard argument is that Britain is an oil producer and that changes in the price of oil therefore affect Britain differently from other countries. In so far as such a change calls for different policy in oil producers from that in oil consumers, it argues against being locked into the same policy. Again the argument is correct. A change in the price of oil is the most obvious although far from the only example of an asymmetric shock.

On the other hand, special characteristics of Britain are sometimes alleged to make the euro more desirable here than elsewhere. The role of the City of London in financial services is said to give Britain much more to gain by being intimately involved with monetary developments. This seems to have much less going for it than the other points. It is difficult to see that effects on one sector of the economy should determine national policy in such an important area. But in any case there is no strong reason to think that London will be disadvantaged in the provision of financial services to the euro area by being located outside it. Financial services is the most globalised industry in the world, largely because it has almost zero transport costs. If this were not true it is difficult to see how Switzerland or for that matter the Cayman Islands, both outside the European Union since it began, could be the successes they are. And indeed, it is no surprise to see that the evidence of experience to date is that London has continued to prosper since the launch of the euro.

Now, Christopher Huhne raises the issue of whether we should expect regulation by the euro members to be constructed to deprive London of its leading position. Whether we should expect, in other words, to be victim of protectionist policy from the European Union.

There is an important issue here, although not, I fear, the one he is raising, and I address it shortly, on page 74.

Should we follow the herd?

It is sometimes said that since most members of the European Union
have joined EMU it is in British interests to join, notwithstanding the
fact that we would rather the plan had never been devised. This argument, always of dubious value, has been shattered by the result of the
Danish referendum. If Denmark can stay outside, Great Britain can.

Furthermore, it is certainly true that, if the euro is economically
damaging to Europe, we should wish that it had never been adopted.
Britain will certainly suffer if there is an economic disaster in continental Europe. But it does not follow from this that conditions will be
worse outside the euro than inside. Outside, at least we have some
opportunity to pursue more balanced economic policies, and policies
more appropriate to whatever position we find ourselves in. We should
not argue that a great mistake has been made in continental Europe
and that therefore it is in our interests to make the same mistake.

A different thought is that most of the European Union has
adopted the Maastricht plan, and if the merits of the proposal are not
substantially different for Britain, there is a paradox in arguing that
Britain should remain outside. The temptation is to assume that an
assessment of the euro's economic merits has been made in continental Europe, that a favourable outcome has resulted in its enthusiastic
adoption, and that a marginally different assessment has led, temporarily at least, to its rejection in Britain. The truth is quite different.
The alleged economic benefits are not the driving force anywhere in
Europe. It is everywhere a matter of political commitment buttressed
by some convenient arguments in economics.

Two things are quite different in Britain. The first is that we have
been much more inclined to debate the issue on its economic merits.
The strong presumption in many minds is that if it is a good idea we
should join, and if it is a bad one we should stay outside. The economic

arguments, once they are properly considered, indicate that the Maastricht plan, if not the whole idea of a single currency, is a bad idea, and in the worst cases a catastrophic one.

The second consideration is that in Britain there is much less general and instinctive support for European integration. Regrettable as some find this, it is a fact of life, and it should quite properly affect our policy. Just how it should affect it is considered in Chapter 6.

Will we lose foreign investment if we remain outside?

An argument along the same general lines – that the euro might be undesirable but since it has gone ahead we should join – is that remaining outside will result in a loss of foreign investment. There is a good deal of scaremongering in this view. In the first place, there is nothing intrinsically special about foreign investment. Investment is investment, whatever its source. British investment earns profit for British investors, foreign for foreign. That is all. Nevertheless, if we do not generate enough investment ourselves, foreign investment is beneficial.

The argument that not joining the euro will reduce foreign investment appears to be that exchange-rate variability makes the future value of an investment uncertain. A continental European investor buying a company in America might find, even if that company is successful, that the value of the investment is, at some point in the future, disappointing because of a fall in the value of the dollar. This, however, is rather a short-termist view. Exchange-rate volatility is considerable, but over the long term – and one presumes it is long-term investment that we are interested in – exchange-rate changes broadly reflect economic fundamentals. Therefore they are about as predictable as those fundamentals. If we think of a firm investing in a fifteen-year project, what will concern it? If it invests and then finds the pound falling, it is earning profits in depreciated currency. (Although it may be earning a lot of such profits, if it is in an export business.) But over the fifteen-year period as a whole what has it to fear? The kind of factor that would lead to the pound being depreciated for a period as long as that is that British inflation is high, or that there is for some reason a collapse of productivity in Britain. In the first case, high inflation means the firm's output will sell for an inflated price. Then, indeed, each pound earned may be worth fewer euros, but many such pounds are earned, and the fall in the exchange rate of the pound gives no reason to regret the investment. On the other hand, if there is a productivity problem, that will be bad for the investor, but it means that the investment decision was poor on its business merits. The bad outcome is not attributable to the fall of the pound. Indeed, it is more likely that it is only that fall which keeps the business solvent at all, and the investor should therefore welcome the fact that British policy has preserved the flexibility to respond appropriately to productivity shocks. Clearly an equivalent argument works for the case of a rise in the pound, and for a British investor considering a euro-area investment.

A true long-term investor makes a calculation on the basis of the size of the British market, the state of labour relations and regulation, the productivity of the workforce, the quality of the transport system and such matters. If these are not as we would wish them, we should rectify those problems. Changing the mechanisms of international adjustment does not affect those things, and is not relevant to the long-term investment decision. The most important of these factors, of course, is the quality of economic management in Britain. If we wish to attract foreign investment, we must wish to remain prosperous. If we wish that, then we must maintain interest rates and fiscal policy appropriate to the British economy. That means keeping the pound.

There has been a hail of scare stories put out by the European Movement apparently intent on persuading us that no one could contemplate an investment outside the euro area, but again and again they have been found to lack factual basis. When the facts are investigated, the companies concerned tend to say, quite clearly, that British non-membership of the euro was not a consideration. There are good reasons for companies to invest in Britain, and fortunately for the world, there are good reason for them to invest elsewhere as well. One cannot construe every case of the latter factors winning as an argument for the euro. The euro-advocates slipped up even more seriously in their attempts to stoke concern at the 'likely' withdrawal of Nissan from Britain 'because of the euro'. But late in January 2001, that company took a decision to remain in Britain for the long term, and to increase production here. As these stories increasingly lose their credibility, the euro-advocates are switching attention to the British share of foreign direct investment into the European Union. The most striking thing about this is how high it remains, despite the absence of any kind of commitment to the euro. If other countries have attracted more in the last few years than they did before, that is no doubt attributable to the slight recovery in their economies. Good for them. It is not a problem for Britain that our partners do well. Overall, the facts tell a very clear story: Britain has remained a magnet for overseas investment and remains far ahead of any other country.

Will we be punished for remaining outside?

An argument which appears slightly more powerful at first sight is that Britain will become subject to reprisals from the rest of Europe designed, in the manner of economic sanctions, to force entry to the euro.[28]

One version of the argument says that a consequence of the monetary policy in the euro area will be to cause the value of the euro to rise in international exchanges, thereby harming the competitiveness of the Euro-area's exporters. Britain and other countries outside would be the beneficiaries of this in the sense that their firms would become more competitive, while European free trade would continue to guarantee free access to continental markets. Sometimes this is called a competitive devaluation by Britain and other outsiders. The unfairness, it is said, of gaining market share because of exchange-rate movements would warrant retaliation, perhaps in the form of tariffs from the euro area.

The first difficulty with the argument is that it is an attempt on the part of advocates of the euro to have their cake and eat it. The basis on which it is said that EMU is desirable is that exchange-rate changes bring little in the way of benefits. This is why we are encouraged to give up the pound. But then, apparently, we are also to believe that exchange-rate changes are powerful enough to warrant retaliatory sanctions. Equally, the basis on which the Maastricht plan is advocated is that the single-minded anti-inflationary policy of the ECB will result in economic prosperity. But, again, this same policy will bring the exchange-rate developments which are to do such harm. If Britain is to have the kind of advantage from being outside that could possibly warrant sanctions, this surely must show that the whole project is undesirable. If advocates of the euro are not willing to take that view, they must give up the sanctions story.

Another question arises about countries which are not members of the European common market? They will presumably be gaining similar advantages. Are they to be subject to trade sanctions as well? Perhaps it is felt that outside the common market their access to European markets is in any case highly restricted, so the euro area has not much to fear. To have this made explicit would be interesting, since the European Union presents itself as a friend of free trade in the world, whereas this outlook clearly implies that it is protectionist with respect to non-members.

Another version of the same kind of story focuses on regulation, and particularly on the financial services sector. In round 1, the Euroenthusiast doom-mongers asserted that Britain would be excluded from the TARGET system for financial settlements. No doubt they all felt a propaganda coup had been scored. In reality, after a few months a perfectly satisfactory agreement was reached giving London access to it.

It is an argument essentially in this character that doubts whether London can be the financial centre for the euro area. The regulations, yet to be created, apparently are likely to discriminate against London, and only membership of the euro can save us. But the question that needs to be considered is that of motive. Why should we fear active discrimination in rule-writing? Since we are told we can escape this fate by joining the euro, it is clearly not a simple matter of national economic advantage: if it benefits France and Germany to discriminate against London, then our membership of the euro is not material. Therefore, it must be that these regulations are proposed as a means of forcing us to join, or at least punishing us for not joining.

That is a very interesting idea, particularly coming from the Euroenthusiasts. Our continental partners, it is proposed, are going to damage the financial efficiency of the whole continent (and perhaps the world) by doing down the most successful centre, as a way of venting their temper at our disinclination to go along with their ill-considered schemes. Further, this is punishment for not joining a scheme where our right to opt-out was specifically agreed at Maastricht and forms part of the Treaty provisions.

Could it be true? I suppose it could, but the consequence would not be a headlong rush to join the euro, but a complete reassessment of what would indeed have to be seen as a mistaken decision to join the European project in the first place. If one were to take this threat of sanctions seriously then it would have to be admitted by the Euroenthusiasts that their argument means that while members of the European Union, we have no national independence of any kind. So, for example, their repeated claims that we need have no fear that membership of the euro will lead to other things (tax harmonisation, pension bail-outs, labour market over-regulation, etc.), would have to be abandoned. We have to agree to whatever is proposed, would be the position they were adopting. Furthermore, the idea of a Treaty, or a solemn commitment, would clearly mean nothing. Our partners agreed to an opt-out; do we not trust them to honour the Treaty?

I find it hard to hold the European Union in this kind of contempt. The Euroenthusiasts may feel we have been sucked into a protection racket worthy of any Chicago mobster of a few decades ago. They may say the European Union will shortly be engaged in trying to break a few economic arms and legs, and perhaps move on to fully fledged protectionism in breach of the Treaty of Rome and numerous world-trade agreements. But if this is what they believe, let them say so clearly. It will be interesting to see whether they still try to adorn their views with the decorations of internationalism, fellow-feeling and the moral imperatives that have up to now characterised the best of the Europeans. For my part, I continue to hold to the view of Europe which makes British membership desirable: it is a society of nations, intent on mutual respect, harmony and the pursuit of common interests. We cannot fear that our closest partners and greatest friends will devote their policy to harming us, in breach of the commitments they have made, but nor, it should be remembered, can we wish to be still closer partners if they do.

5 Can the Treaty be improved?

Will it be all right on the night?

When confronted with the undesirability of the Maastricht rules, an increasingly frequent response of advocates of the euro is to argue that there is nothing to worry about because if Britain joins the rules will either be ignored or changed. The European Union, they say, is a pragmatic organisation and the commitment to making the euro work is great, so things will be sorted out. In other words, it will be all right on the night.

This is a peculiar argument for advocates of European integration to use. It involves disowning the Treaty they advocate and admitting that it is a bad Treaty, and again implies that we should presume our European partners incapable of making a binding agreement. Thus it is said the Treaty is only a scrap of paper and no basis for policy.

More important than its peculiarity, however, is the fact that this is a risky argument. Several considerations suggest we should not rely on good sense prevailing. For one thing, Christopher Huhne agrees that the Treaty 'may' need amendment, particularly with regard to the fiscal provisions. But no one will suppose that his consent is enough to determine the policy of the European Union. Indeed, his view is not even shared among the British euro-advocates. Lord Leon Brittan, for example, described the Stability Pact as 'an essential part of EMU'.[29] Taking a wider view, there has been rather little sign of the attitude that reform is imminent. The details of the Stability Pact were agreed only in 1997, well after the folly of the Maastricht rules had been exposed. By then it was apparent that European governments' expenditure cuts were inhibiting recovery in their own countries as well as in those of their neighbours, but that did not stop a Pact requiring fines being agreed.

As to monetary policy, the culture of price stability at all costs is deeply ingrained in the Bundesbank and has been inherited by the European Central Bank (ECB), which is so closely modelled on it. Indeed, for a long time, this approach was highly successful in West Germany. The fact that it has had unfortunate results since German unification should be a double warning: first, that the Maastricht policy is a bad policy; and second, that the policy will nevertheless be followed. No one forced such a damaging policy on the Bundesbank, but it adopted it, the French followed suit and so did most of the European Union. What is supposed to be different now that EMU has begun?

Still worse than the facts that the lessons have not been learned, and that arguments for a different policy framework do not command general assent, is that there are powerful vested interests supporting the Maastricht framework. Central banks should not be expected to give up their independence easily, and they will constitute a powerful lobby to preserve the Maastricht framework. Many businesses, rightly or wrongly, perceive themselves as beneficiaries of a low inflation policy. In Germany the terms of the Treaty are widely seen as safeguarding low inflation against the desires of other countries to pursue a different policy. To change the objectives or remove the independence of the ECB requires the unanimous agreement of all the signatories of the Treaty. There is no prospect of this. Indeed, it is difficult to imagine many governments making such a proposal because it would inevitably appear to be an attempt actually to raise inflation. The rules are foolish ones, but it is not so easy to propose their amendment, however balanced and sensible a policy a government wishes to pursue, without seeming to advocate irresponsibility.

There have been a few rumblings from some of the governments embarking on EMU to the effect that the rules of the Stability Pact should be relaxed, but little comfort should be taken from this. In the first place, it can hardly be said that the mild relaxations being proposed represent a reassessment of the role of fiscal policy in economic management, which is what is required. It has also become apparent that the ECB and others who see themselves as custodians of the 'wisdom' of Maastricht are determined to resist these moves as strongly as possible. The great problem with the Treaty is, of course, as with central bank independence, that it puts European law very much on their side.

There is also an internal logic of the Maastricht framework which argues against even contemplating changes in the Treaty. This is where the doctrine of credibility is so important. When people are in the frame of mind of thinking that only binding commitments can bring the all-important private-sector expectations into the desired position, revoking these commitments appears certain to damage economic outcomes. The alleged danger of losing credibility is bound to be invoked if any proposal for relaxing the Maastricht rules gains even the mildest support among European governments.

Lastly, there is room for significant doubt as to whether the European Union really is so pragmatic and able to change bad rules as advocates of the euro, and integration more generally, assume. One example will suffice. The Common Agricultural Policy, decades after it was created, continues to raise food prices, distort markets, wreak environmental havoc, dominate the EU budget, damage the standing of Europe in the eyes of the rest of the world, endanger world trading arrangements and provoke continual discord between the members of the Union. When is this going to change? Can we afford decades of the Maastricht rules?

When the euro-advocates can point to a broadly based change of heart, when they can show that the vested interests supporting the Maastricht arrangement – the 'independent' central bank among them – have been overcome, when they have actually changed the rules, that will be the appropriate time to consider what should be done. There is no prospect of the euro-advocates agreeing to this approach, but of course, that is because there is no prospect of such changes occurring.

A European fiscal policy

A different kind of change in the Treaty has been suggested: the creation of a European fiscal policy. The argument, made properly, accepts that EMU will indeed create unemployment in some countries, and suggests that this could be mitigated to a degree with fiscal policy in those countries, except that the Stability Pact makes this difficult, if not impossible. The solution therefore is a federal fiscal policy, which will also have the effect of taxing richer countries and transferring the money to poorer ones. This may go some way towards moderating differences in business cycles.[30]

From a certain perspective this proposal clearly has merit, independently of the discussion of EMU, although it is difficult to see how it could be welcomed by anyone opposed to political union. It would necessitate granting powers to an EU institution either directly to tax citizens or to assess taxes on member governments and leave it to them to raise the money and hand it over. Equally, of course, it is difficult to see that such a development can be envisaged by those supporters of EMU who continue to deny that it is a significant step towards political union. It cannot logically be believed that monetary union involves no significant steps towards political union, and that to be successful monetary union needs a federal fiscal policy, and also that monetary union will in fact be successful. Yet this appears to be the position of some advocates of the euro.

Others, however, have started to describe the creation of a European fiscal policy as inevitable. From the perspective of making EMU a success it would certainly be an improvement on the policy framework contained in the Maastricht Treaty. But it is not clear that it will be acceptable. Germans will understand that they are being asked to pay, and others will expect to receive, but such a Treaty amendment would require unanimity. In the event of Britain joining the euro, what do we suppose will be the attitude of the British government? We can hardly expect an opt-out from a device which is alleged to be essential to the success of the euro, but we would expect on average to be contributors to, rather than recipients from, such a device, if not immediately, then certainly after the admission of the countries of central and eastern Europe.

From the point of view of the management of the European economy, a federal fiscal policy is certainly better than what we are offered. But if advocates of the euro wish to stand by the claim that the European Union is pragmatic, and problems are solved as they develop, they should face the fact that the improvement required in the Treaty is not the addition of more supranational power, but the scrapping of the policy framework and its replacement by a balanced attitude to the objectives of economic policy and the methods of pursuing them. This is simply not on the horizon. If it ever comes about, we should reconsider British participation. But at present the European economies have been blighted by the same attitude as is enshrined in the Treaty, and we should give no credence whatsoever to the hope that all will mysteriously change now that the euro is under way.

6 The political consequences of the euro

Is the euro intended to promote political union?

Undoubtedly, those who have been most energetic in advancing the euro see the project as leading to political union. Why else would Jacques Santer, at the time president of the European Commission, have described the finalising of the original membership of the euro as 'a landmark date on which European integration took on a new momentum'?[31] Indeed, it is difficult to find continental politicians who express any doubt about this presumption, although in Britain many, even among advocates of political union, have been reluctant to see the euro as promoting further steps along that road. Nevertheless, this is exactly what the Treaty of Rome calls for. The stated goal of European integration is 'ever closer union'. British politicians, and occasionally continental ones, advancing particular steps have found it in their interests to deny that each step is part of a larger project, but it is.

Why supporters of political union should reject the euro

The fact that monetary union is a step towards political union is not in itself a reason to oppose it, since there are those who genuinely favour political union. For them to oppose the euro is difficult because it is so symbolic of their goal. Nevertheless, the truth must be that a monetary union which is economically damaging will retard, if not destroy, the integration process.

The danger to the European project arises from the fact that recessions, and economic distress in general, are rarely conducive to internationalism. Although a perfectly respectable case could be made that times of economic failure are the times when most is to be gained from openness and trade, to imagine that these are ever in practice likely to follow from economic failure is foolish.

It would be remarkable if anyone were to claim that the successes achieved by parties of the extreme right in several European countries, most noticeably in France, are unrelated to the economic failure of recent years. Of course unemployment at persistently high levels has bred racism in France. The outlook of these groups is one which the vast majority of British supporters of the euro would find objectionable, but why has their support grown so much as the Maastricht Treaty recession has developed? Why has neo-Nazism returned to the German political stage? Why have extremist movements enjoyed such success in so many countries?

Whilst the experience of preparing for the euro was bad enough, the situation is now worse. First, an undesirable policy being imposed from a foreign city, with the national government having no control, since it no longer controls the policy instrument, will be politically provocative. It should be remembered that it is inevitable that policy interests among countries will differ at some point in the future. The estimates of the costs of this have wholly disregarded the issue of political resentment building up. Yet it is impossible to imagine unemployment rising in a poorer member of the euro area because richer members are suffering mild inflation without such resentments. Equally, it is hard to imagine inflation rising much in Germany without corresponding resentments. These resentments will count against the idea of Europe. They will be aggravated, moreover, by the unaccountability and lack of legitimacy of the European institutions which will be imposing the policy.

Christopher Huhne suggests that I am overdoing this concern because interest rates will be much less politically sensitive than they have been in the past or are in Britain. Personally, I doubt it. I suspect that when unfavourable decisions are handed down by remote policymakers, that in itself will attract more political resentment. But in any case, concern should not focus on interest rates themselves. The primary concern is about unemployment. One does not need a detailed understanding of economic theory to appreciate that policy set in a foreign city is harming one's wellbeing. Nor does one need a highly developed sense of political theory to resent government welfare cuts in a recession imposed by the Stability Pact. The claim that when these things happen resentment will follow is certainly to some degree speculative. But I would much prefer it if the European Union had left them entirely in the realm of speculation. Unfortunately, it has insisted on testing them. No one should welcome that.

Second, whatever ill effects the Maastricht plan has on European businesses, it should be a great opportunity for political entrepreneurship. We cannot expect adverse economic developments imposed from foreign cities by unelected bankers not to lead to the creation of political movements specifically to oppose these things. Such movements will probably hold politically objectionable views along with their economically more sensible ones. A general disapproval of European integration and internationalism is likely, accompanied by a tendency to blame foreigners and racial minorities for economic failure. These political movements, which are already evident in many countries, will prosper in the policy environment of the Maastricht Treaty. They are also likely to profit from the attitude taken in so much advocacy of Maastricht, that democracy is in any case a flawed form of government and that we are better off handing over our basic economic interests to bankers and other appointed experts to do as they please. It is an unfortunate moment to be seeking to inculcate such a culture.

It is not necessary to go as far as Professor Martin Feldstein, who suggested that the threat of war between west European countries could be revived.[32] The danger, in its mildest form, is merely that the standing of the integration project will be damaged by the perception that national economic distress is being imposed by outsiders. In a slightly worse version, there will be pressure for trade protectionism to safeguard jobs. Thus could European free trade lose the legitimacy it has progressively gained. In such circumstances, there is no doubt that some political group will find it in its interests to advocate withdrawal from the euro, and perhaps from the European Union. If the economic conditions are bad enough this position will prove attractive, whatever its theoretical limitations. In any case, it is difficult to imagine that the European Union as a whole will not be pushed in a protectionist direction by such developments, threatening the world trading system.[33]

The likelihood of these developments does not depend on the introduction of the euro being disadvantageous overall. I have argued that it will be damaging and recessionary for the whole of Europe and for the world at large, and this will certainly make matters worse. But whatever happens there will be losers somewhere at some points. It is in those places at those times that the fabric of European integration, and perhaps European democracy, will begin to unravel. The basic reason is that the political process will not support damaging policy imposed from a different country by unaccountable bankers.

It is a sad fact, therefore, that symbolism has triumphed over sense in most of the European Union. In Britain, however, the consequences of a mistaken decision to join the euro might be even worse. And that is now the crucial policy issue before us.

Why British integration-enthusiasts should be even firmer in opposing British membership of the euro

The same basic issues, of course, arise in Britain as they do in the rest of Europe, except that we would be wise to be particularly cautious about the danger of unsuitable policy since history suggests a tendency for British interest rates to diverge from those on the continent.

But there are three further considerations, each of which appears at first sight to make a case for Britain joining the euro, but which taken together in fact make the opposite case. One is that, however undesirable it may be, it has been done. It is too late to argue against the whole proposal. The second is that it is said that British influence in Europe in general depends on our participation in the central schemes adopted there. Finally, a point which is hard to separate fully from either of these is that British influence on the integration process has already been damaged by reluctance to participate and we should do everything we can to avoid further such damage.

In fact, however, the value of these arguments in making the case for British participation is nil. Indeed, properly considered, the issues raised argue for our non-participation. And this point, it should be noted, has nothing to do with a disregard for the opinion of the rest of the world, or with British nationalism, but rather follows from a calm assessment of the issue from the point of view of the internationalist and the sincere integrationist.

The first crucial point is that it is an illusion that EMU can be implemented and that will be the end of the story; that it will be the end of the integrationist project. There may be a few in Britain who imagine it is the end, but that defies common sense and the history of the European Union, as well as being readily contradicted by a reading of the European pages of any national newspaper – there are many proposals currently in the air for further integration.

It is worth recalling that the last major step of integration, variously known as the single European market, the internal market programme or just '1992', was agreed by Britain and the others with no commitment to monetary union or other further steps of comparable importance. Much of the advocacy of 1992 centred on estimates of economic gains popularised for the European Commission by Emerson and others.[34] Before the programme was even scheduled to be complete, Euroenthusiasts were advocating EMU on the basis that a single market needs a single currency, a consideration which had been notably absent from the discussion of the benefits of the single market. Again a propaganda document was produced by the Commission estimating economic benefits. Many of its arguments flatly contradicted ones that had been advanced in the earlier book, but no matter, the earlier one had served its purpose.[35] The British government had a legal right to veto the EMU plan but did not do so. The other countries reacted to the possibility of a veto by creating the device of an opt-out: the rest would go ahead, but Britain would be allowed to remain outside.

The next move in the game, which is the stage we have now reached, is for the Euroenthusiasts to assert, first, that since the euro is going ahead, we ought to join for the sake of our standing in Europe; and second, that no important further steps are entailed, and if any are suggested Britain will have a legal right to veto them. Further, we are assured that a benefit of joining will be enhanced influence in Europe.

But what do we suppose would really happen? First, if Britain were to join the euro, far from establishing us firmly as the leading nation in the continent, it would in fact be treated as a signal that the next major step was due. Exactly what that step would be is hard to say, but a significant move towards tax harmonisation is a likely candidate. What are we to say when that proposal is made? We can veto it, seek an opt-out, or agree. In the first case, the hope of finding ourselves at the heart of Europe is gone in an instant. We remain the awkward partner. But we are then the awkward partner that joined monetary union under a delusion – the political benefit we were promised does not exist. In the second case – of an opt-out – we are put back in the current position. Still awkward, still with the Euroenthusiasts, presumably, telling us that we cannot afford to be awkward and must opt-in. But then the price will be some other proposal, and the same problem again. In the third case, we can agree to tax harmonisation. Down that road, perhaps, lies the end of the British awkwardness. It is in our power to become the leading advocates of integration, and if we do, we shall surely find respect among those on the continent who take the same view. But the crucial thing is that it is only down the road of full-hearted enthusiasm that such a result can be found. There is simply no hope of our finding ourselves at the top table of Europe because we have ceased to be awkward about EMU and become awkward instead about the next item on the agenda.

What we need at this point, then, is a clear account from the advocates of the euro of how they intend to respond to such further proposals. Some, surely, are true European integrationists, for whom the full powers of central government being located in Brussels is the goal. That is an entirely respectable position, particularly if one admits to it.

For the most part, however, what we get is a statement that further integration is not necessary, with the additional assurance that we still have a veto, and that other countries have also recently rejected certain proposals. (There is no implication that they have taken a permanent decision to abandon the general project of ever closer union.) Well, of course it is not necessary to integrate further. That was the case with monetary union, and more or less every proposal for European integration that there has ever been. The question is not about necessity but rather, when it is proposed, are we to agree? Before the argument on improving British influence in Europe can be worth a bean, this question must be answered. And the answer, furthermore, must be that we are to become true enthusiasts, ready to take the lead, ready to agree, ready if others will it, to give up national independence altogether.

Perhaps we are, perhaps we should be. I should be most disappointed, myself, to give up the European dream, although it must be said, it looks ever more likely to remain a dream. This is one reason we would be better off abandoning debate over specific issues, of which the euro is an important one, but only one, and attending to the problem of achieving a consensus on the matters of principle that must frame a desirable Europe. Larry Siedentop's efforts, for example, to turn attention in that direction, are surely to be welcomed.[36] In any case, the crucial point about the further developments planned by many in the European Union is not that they inevitably, and unstoppably will be forced on us if we join the euro. The point is about the logic of the argument that would have us join. The hope that we can have improved influence – whatever that means precisely – is the purest wishful thinking unless it is imagined that we are also to welcome much else.

At present, it seems that there is almost no one arguing for the adoption of the euro on the basis that we should then be ready to advocate further major steps. Perhaps Britain has reached a degree of euroscepticism where there is no one who supports such a position. Perhaps those who do support it are keeping quiet. Or perhaps they are trying to present the euro as a stand-alone option, unconnected to other issues.

The danger, from the point of view of the integrationist, however, is not merely that one of the benefits alleged to follow from the euro is not available. It is deeper than that, because pushing the euro on Britain risks damaging our standing in Europe, not just leaving it unchanged.

In the first place, so complete is the euro-advocates' denial of the possibility of having further measures forced on us, that it must be supposed that some of them at least will be on the sceptic side when, in the event of our joining the euro, we come to debate them. That will make it even more apparent to Europe and the world that we are not true integrationists, and we will find even less respect among those who are.

Against this, we should consider the hope that success of the euro will itself erode scepticism about integration in general. The point is quite fair: we may come to welcome further integration, and if we do, there is not much to be said against it. Something like this has always been part of the plan of the integrationists. They have felt that small steps could lead to great things by gradually giving the project legitimacy. But despite the theoretical appeal of the proposition, as a matter of fact, it rather clearly does not work. If it did, then after thirty years in the European Union the British would, on the whole, be more enthusiastic about the project than we were. But on the contrary, there is great resistance to monetary union itself, and to the political union which is believed to be following it.

But the general idea behind this argument should not be dismissed. To some degree, surely the success or otherwise of integration, and particularly the extent to which it fulfils the promises made for it, are instrumental in achieving support for further moves, or even sticking with the moves already made. In this connection it should be noted that British support for European integration is now low, and fragile. Indeed, one does hear talk of withdrawal. Some of the euro-advocates have even suggested that the true agenda of those who believe the euro is based on bad economics, is to see Britain withdraw. Why so many of those now opposed to the euro have previously supported European integration is a question they ignore. But low and fragile support for membership of the European Union, regrettable as it is, remains a fact of British politics today. The question for the true integration-enthusiasts, as well as those who see the euro as the last major step they are inclined to support, is what will happen if Britain joins and bad results follow? The economic risks are clear: a divergence of interest, about which the European Central Bank can do nothing; an excessive concern for reducing inflation at whatever cost, about which it could do a lot, but probably will not; or a fine descending on us, voted by our partner governments. I have argued that resentment and opposition to integration will follow from these things in any country. But sceptical Britain must be the most fertile ground.[37]

It can only make matters worse if we have been induced to join by false pretences. There are some now, although it infuriates the true enthusiasts to have to admit it, who feel they were conned into joining the European Economic Community. But what attitude can there be if we ever find ourselves in the position where we have reluctantly joined the euro, perhaps after a narrow vote in a referendum, perhaps also a referendum where the terms of engagement were not seen as fair? Add to this the possibility that instrumental in joining were arguments quickly exposed as false to the effect that we would not have further measures thrust upon us. Down this road, surely, lies the possibility of a collapse of the consensus that has seen Britain a secure member of the European Union.

The right way to develop the European Union is to build the institutions on the foundation of their legitimacy in the public mind. To await, therefore, the genuine feeling of the peoples of Europe that their interests are sufficiently interlocked so that it is appropriate to have one economic policy for the whole continent. The hope that imposing a single policy will engender its own legitimacy contradicts common sense, and furthermore takes a huge gamble, not just with our economic fortunes but with our political institutions and support for the project of integration as well. These things apply most of all in Britain.

So, those who earnestly hope for a United States of Europe should have opposed monetary union from the moment its nature became clear. At the very least they should have insisted on a policy framework which balanced the many interests in economic policymaking, rather than presuming even the slightest inflation to be not merely the greatest but the only evil. On those terms, whether a role could be found for EMU as a means of enhancing the legitimacy of the European Union might have become a debatable issue. They missed that chance, but they can still act properly with respect to Britain. They can still see that the arguments must be squarely put, the risks appreciated, the requirements of influence in Europe clearly stated, and if they cannot win support on that basis, it serves their goals to oppose British membership of the euro themselves.

7 **Conclusion**

Monetary union has been the dream of the Euroenthusiasts, in Britain as elsewhere, since the outset. At last at Maastricht in 1991 it seemed the dream had come true. There was a commitment by eleven countries to a specific timetable leading to a common currency. This plan has now been implemented, and many in Britain fear that our standing in Europe will again be damaged by delay in joining.

It is true that much that the European Union has done has been good for Britain, as it has for other countries. In many respects it could have been better if we had participated more eagerly in the good European schemes at an earlier stage. But it makes no sense to join a monetary union now because we regret not joining a customs union in 1958.

Despite the benefits of Europe there have been, and the greater ones there might have been, the Euroenthusiasts need to rethink. The estimated benefits of the euro, small as they are, have probably been exaggerated, and the economic costs of monetary union have been much understated. Everything points towards the desirability of different policies in different countries. Even in the United States, a much more closely integrated economic area than the European Union, different regions experience different conditions.

To some extent the need for different policies is mitigated by labour mobility. This does much to account for the success of the United States. But Europe is far from having the same degree of labour mobility as the United States and will progressively move further from it as more countries join the European Union, introducing more linguistic and cultural diversity. So we cannot expect European monetary union closely to resemble that of the United States.

THE ARGUMENTS AGAINST THE EURO

Of course, it is only monetary policy that must be the same throughout a monetary union. To some extent appropriate fiscal policy can compensate for the damage done by inappropriately unified monetary policy. It can never fully compensate, but it can mitigate. This is also probably part of the story of US success, but again things are not the same in Europe. There is no federal fiscal policy. National fiscal policy might do the job, but is constrained by the very agreement creating the monetary union. So again Europe faces the problem of differential developments without having the means to deal with them.

There is more. The Maastricht rules create a permanent and unqualified prioritisation of the control of inflation and place policy in the hands of central bankers, who are by intention less accountable than any central banker, or probably any public servant of any kind, has ever been in a democracy. This is no accident. It is a deliberate response to the doctrine of policy credibility. Revocable commitments can be revoked, therefore only irrevocable ones are persuasive. Thus the statutes of the European Central Bank can be changed only by the unanimous agreement of every national parliament, and in some cases national referenda as well.

In general, the Euroenthusiasts respond that it will be all right on the night. Never mind that the Treaty is a bad Treaty, Europe is still a sensible environment for achieving good policy. There is nothing to fear. But is this true? What about the Common Agricultural Policy and the Common Fisheries Policy? When will this sensible organisation resolve these issues? Why did the British budgetary dispute take so long to resolve in the 1980s? Why has there been such a failure of the European Union to assert itself in foreign and security affairs, even within the European continent?

More strikingly, why was the Treaty written this way in the first place if it is agreed to be so foolish? I wonder how many of the Euroenthusiasts are among those who are proud of not having read the Maastricht Treaty. But for any who have read it, there are some extremely lucid parts and most of them relate to the importance of central bank independence, the absolute prioritisation of price stability, the restriction of fiscal policy and the exclusion of elected representatives of the people from the policymaking process. These are all the things, in other words, which the complacent advocates say we should suppose it does not mean.

Since the Treaty was agreed, unemployment rates all over the continent have been at levels unprecedented since the Great Depression. Why? Because of world recession, perhaps? No. The United States boomed for most of the period, as did most of South-east Asia until recently. Because of the burden of supporting East Germany? But could a state a fraction of the size of West Germany have dragged the whole of the largest economic area in the world into a decade-long recession? Hardly. The cause of the great European recession of the 1990s has been that independent central banks, obsessed by their 'credibility', and budget-cutting governments have been implementing the Maastricht policy rules since the Treaty was signed. Interest rates have been too high, the Deutschmark and all the currencies tied to it have been overvalued and government expenditure has been inappropriately cut. Europe has suffered the Maastricht Recession.

So let no one say that the Maastricht policy framework is a good one. Even if Europe was, early in 2001, at last enjoying a period of relative prosperity, the evidence is clear: the Maastricht policy framework is a bad one. A couple of years of falling unemployment do not rewrite the history of a decade. But let no one say either that the framework is a bad one but there is nothing to worry about, since it will not be followed. It has been followed. Disaster or not, we can see clearly the danger that the policy will be followed since it has been for so long. The minimum condition of British participation in EMU should be that it be established on sound principles of economic management and democratic accountability. There really need be no further discussion until this is achieved.

But there is more to worry about. European institutions lack legitimacy. These institutions have direct control of some of the most fundamental determinants of economic well-being for most of the continent. And they have an impossible task. It is inconceivable that the same policy will suit all parts of the euro area all the time. Even if policy is not in future a deflationary disaster for the whole continent as it has been recently, it is sure to be deflationary for some parts at some times. As Christopher Huhne says, the area stretches from Helsinki to Cadiz and Sligo to Brindisi. Somewhere, sometime, there will be recession while the rest of the euro area booms. Then interest rates will rise for the whole area and the country or region in recession will suffer.

Some consideration of the political consequences of this circumstance is now more urgent than ever. There will be deep resentment and it will be a resentment for which there is no useful outlet. Not protest to the national government, which has given up its powers; not protest to the real economic government in Frankfurt, since even if it were inclined to recognise an objective other than price stability, it can do nothing for one region in recession while others boom.

These dilemmas already arise in our existing countries, but we have three essential antidotes. We have some degree of labour mobility and reasonable fiscal redistribution. These things are not always enough, but they do help. We also have deeply rooted feelings of the identity of the nation states. This makes it acceptable, in most cases, that there is one policy for the whole country. There are a few exceptions to this. Separatist movements exist in parts of several European countries, and this is surely a most persuasive argument that the European Union cannot expect to escape such movements when policy starts to damage some part to the benefit of others. It is widely questioned in Scotland whether Scottish economic interests have been served by government from London. How can it be doubted that the same question will be asked about government from Frankfurt by whoever suffers from its policy? In Britain, the fears for the legitimacy of the project are the greatest. Full-hearted support will surely be lacking for a long time to come. But if the careless Euroenthusiasts, and those who seek their own political advancement in the project, lever us into it anyway, it will be an even rougher road to travel. As one who has had high hopes for European integration, and for enthusiastic British participation in it, I find that path unconscionable.

I fear, too, that the political movements arising from these circumstances will not all be in most things moderate. High, persistent unemployment breeds racism, not just separatism. And it is objectionable organisations which will benefit from the Maastricht policy. No doubt they will also benefit from the fact that so many people – in our own country, amazingly, even Liberal Democrats among them – have now followed the Bundesbank's lead in denying the role of democratic accountability in economic governance. It may then, if generally adverse circumstances develop or divergences between different country's interests become too great, not be inappropriate to doubt the hold of liberal democracy on the European political process. This is the greatest fear of all.

So Europe is in a mess. What should it have done? Turn back, having come so far, and look foolish, or go on, accepting the consequences? In the best case the consequences are mild. Some transactions costs are saved and fortune favours the project with a world environment conducive to painless price stability and a European one without too many serious divergences of interest. It should have been obvious to turn back, because in any circumstances less favourable than these a heavy economic price is paid. The dreamers continue to dream that the economic price can be paid and somehow the European Union will become ever more popular, but it can only be a dream, not reality.

But turning back was, apparently, impossible. The ghost of the Werner plan haunted the project, too many important individuals staked too much on it, and it had to be carried out. In Britain we are luckier. We are not committed and in every way we are entitled to remain outside the euro. This will not allow us to avoid all damage, but with sensible, balanced policy, it will allow us to avoid much of it. Nor is it Euroscepticism which should keep us out. Eurosceptics have no

difficulty in knowing that they wish to remain outside the euro. .
quite logical. But it is the Euroenthusiasts who should fear Maast
the most; the Euroenthusiasts who should regret that it has come so
far; and, above all, the Euroenthusiasts who should be most determined in opposing British participation in a bad European project.

Notes

1   Gros and Thygesen (1991).

2   This rule contained a fudge factor which allowed some flexibility in the application of the 60 per cent cut-off. It proved to be essential in getting the show on the road.

3   The expressions 'interest rates in Germany' or 'German interest rates' mean the interest rates that apply to Deutschmarks, not the rate that applies to any money which happens to be in Germany. It is possible to open a dollar account in London and the interest rate will vary more or less with American rates, not British ones; it is an 'American interest rate'.

4   Emerson *et al.* (1992).

5   Emerson *et al.* (1992), especially pages 75–7. They emphasise, for example, the benefits that would come from more European involvement in environmental policy, the desirability of a 'free internal energy market in electricity' and several other things with no connection to monetary union.

6   Emerson *et al.* (1992), pages 66–8.

7   It is 'in a certain sense' because their methodology is rather confusing. It would certainly be a mistake to suggest that they showed that there was a cost to businesses equivalent to transportation costs across 1,780 miles. What they showed was that the correlation in price *movements* between similar goods on each side of the border was the same as that between goods in two cities 1,780 miles apart on the same side. Exactly how one should interpret that statistic is none too clear.

8   The European Commission's remarks are in Emerson *et al.* (1988), page 73. The (British) Competition Commission's report, 'New Cars:

A report on the supply of new motor cars within the UK'; House of Commons Command No. 4660, was published on 10/04/00. A summary can be read at the Competition Commission's website: http://www.competition-commission.org.uk/

9   The data can be found in the reverse half of the book on page 31.

10 Emerson *et al.* (1992) pages 83–4. When these opinions are not favourable, as for example over the minimum wage or indeed the Social Chapter more generally, strangely little is heard about them from this source.

11 Fourteenth Report of the Trade and Industry Select Committee of the House of Commons, 16 November 2000, paragraph 57. The whole document can be read at http://www. parliament.the-stationery-office.co.uk/pa/cm199900/cmselect/cmtrdind/755/75502.htm, but the content is no more for the faint-hearted than its address.

12 In Baimbridge, Burkitt and Whyman (2000), page 174.

13 Paragraph 57.

14 *Daily Telegraph*, 22 June 1999.

15 *Financial Times*, 25 January 2001.

16 Emerson *et al.* (1992), page 138.

17 One can certainly imagine some other way of controlling inflation. Higher taxes would be one way, but in the recent British case they would have to be very much higher, and if this is the plan of the advocates of the euro, they are none too open about it.

18 *Financial Times*, 17 March 1999.

19 According to the OECD 'Economic Outlook', there were thirteen such falls in the twenty-nine countries of the OECD in the period 1981–98. That is thirteen out of 551 observations.

20 Article 2 of the stability pact allows member states about to be fined to make 'observations', but this does not seem to change the basic position. It is written in European legalese and is none too clear, but that article says, in part:

    2. The Commission when preparing a report under Article 104c (3) shall, as a rule consider an excess over the reference

value resulting from a severe economic downturn to be exceptional only if there is an annual fall of real GDP of at least 2 per cent.

3. The Council when deciding, according to Article 104c (6), whether an excessive deficit exists, shall in its overall assessment take into account any observations made by the Member State showing that an annual fall of real GDP of less than 2 per cent is nevertheless exceptional in the light of further supporting evidence, in particular on the abruptness of the downturn or on the accumulated loss of output relative to past trends.

21 The OECD 'Economic Outlook' records the fall in 1992 as 2 per cent, the British government's own 'Blue Book' has it as only 1.9 per cent. So on the British numbers there was no fall as large as 2 per cent. (And only twelve, not thirteen, in the whole OECD – see footnote 16.)

22 By, I am embarrassed to report, Forder (1998a), and the point was in fact acknowledged by *The Economist* of 27 February 1999.

23 Emerson *et al.* (1992), page 107.

24 The argument is made more fully by Bibow (2000).

25 There are many other theoretical errors in supposing that the credibility problem, if there is one, can be solved by central bank independence, and I confess to having gone into them in some detail in Forder (1998b).

26 All the fiscal deficit numbers for this discussion come from OECD (1998). The comments on French budgetary policy come from OECD (1994), (1995) and (1997). These are the OECD's reports on policy and economic developments in France.

27 And, one might add, even if we are committed to only looking at the most recent information, it does not make a convincing case that all is well in the euro area. At the time of writing, German unemployment has risen in each of the last two months, and the Italians are again facing an imminent confrontation with the European Commission

over their fiscal profligacy – they are still, in fact, running a deficit even in a period of fast growth (*Financial Times*, 20 March, 2001, p37).

28 The first version of this argument was most famously advanced by Padoa-Schioppa (1996) Chapter 6. Another version is to be found in John Edmonds in Bainbridge, Burkitt and Whyman (2000, p193). The idea that regulations will be designed to damage us is another variation on the theme.

29 Brittan (2000), page 187.

30 This idea received an academic from Sala-i-Martin and Sachs (1992), but in one form or another has been a common theme of Continental Euroenthusiasm. For example Jean-Claude Trichet said 'The Council of Ministers will have far more power over the budgets of member states than the federal government in the United States has over the budget of Texas.' *The European*, 7–13 December 1998.

31 European Commission (1998).

32 Feldstein (1997).

33 A possibility I have explored more fully in Forder (1998c).

34 Emerson *et al.* (1988).

35 Emerson *et al.* (1992). The major contradictions were highlighted by Peter Oppenheimer and his co-author (1996).

36 Siedentop (2000).

37 Which is not to say, incidentally, that Britain is the most fertile ground for the objectionable politics I expect to be associated with such movements. That is a different question, and I have high hopes of the strength of our democratic tradition, despite the attempts of the advocates of government by experts to undermine it. But as a place to establish a secessionist party, one must think that a Britain harmed by the euro would be the best.

References

Alberola, E. and Tyrvainen, T. (1998) 'Is there scope for inflation differentials in EMU? An empirical evaluation of the Balassa-Samuelson model in EMU countries', Discussion Papers, 15, Economics Department, Bank of Finland.

Andersen Consulting (1998) *Business, Britain and Europe: the first 25 years*, European Movement, London.

Arrowsmith, J. (1998, July) 'Large scale EMU: the May council decisions and implications for monetary policy', *National Institute Economic Review*, London.

Arrowsmith, J. (ed.) (1998) 'Thinking the unthinkable about EMU: coping with turbulence between 1998 and 2002', National Institute Occasional Paper No. 51, London.

Arrowsmith, J., Barrell, R. and Taylor, C. (1998, October) 'Managing the Euro in a Tri-polar World', paper presented at the 21st colloquium of the Société Universitaire Européene de Recherches Financières, Frankfurt (mimeo).

Bainbridge, M., Burkitt, B. and Whymar, P. (2000) *The Impact of the Euro*, Macmillan, London.

Balassa, B. (1964, December) 'The Purchasing Power Parity doctrine: a reappraisal', *Journal of Political Economy*.

Baldwin, R. (1989, October) 'The growth effects of 1992', *Economic Policy*.

Baldwin, R. (1990) 'On the microeconomics of EMU', in Commission of the European Communities, *One Market, One Money*.

Bayoumi, T. (1989, August), 'Saving Investment correlations: immobile capital, government policy or endogenous behaviour?', IMF Working Paper No. 89/66.

Bayoumi, T. and Masson, P. R. (1996) 'Fiscal flows in the United States and Canada: Lessons for monetary union in Europe', *European Economic Review*.

Bibow, J. (2000) 'Making EMU work: some lessons from the 1990s', Discussion Paper No. 53, University of Hamburg Fachbereich Wirtschaftswissensihafter, Institut für Statistik und Okonometrie.

Brandner, P., Diepalek, L. and Schuberth, H. (1998) 'Structural budget deficits and sustainability of fiscal positions in the European Union', Working Paper No. 26, Oesterreichische NationalBank, Vienna.

Brittan, Lord Leon (2000) *A Diet of Brussels*, Little, Brown & Co., London.

Bureau Européen des Unions de Consommateurs (BEUC) (April, 1988) *Transferts de l'Argent a l'intérieur de la CEE*.

Canzoneri, M., Diba, B. and Eudey, G. (1996, June) 'Trends in European productivity and real exchange rates: implications for the Maastricht convergence criteria and for inflation targets after EMU', Centre for Economic Policy Research, Discussion Paper No. 1417.

Centre for Economics and Business Research for the Confederation of British Industry (1992) *The impact of UK attitudes to the EU on inward investment into the UK*.

Centre for Economics and Business Research for the Corporation of London (1998) *The City's Importance to the European Union Economy*.

Commission of the European Communities (1977, April) *Report of the Study Group on the role of Public Finance in European Integration* (The MacDougall report), Brussels.

Currie, D. (1997) *The pros and cons of EMU*, Economist Intelligence Unit, London.

Davidson, I. (1998) *Jobs and the Rhineland Model*, Federal Trust.

Deutsch, R. (1998, January) *The advent of a true euro corporate and high yield market*, Merrill Lynch.

Dornbusch, R., Favero, C. and Giavazzi, F. (1998, April) 'Immediate challenges for the European Central Bank', *Economic Policy*, No. 26.

Eichengreen, B. (1996, December) 'EMU: an outsider's perspective', Center for International and Development Economics Research (CIDER), Working Paper No. C96-079, University of California, Berkeley.

Eichengreen, B. and Wyplosz, C. (1998, April) 'The Stability Pact: more than a minor nuisance?', *Economic Policy*.

Emerson, M. and Huhne, C. (1991) *The Ecu report*, London.

Emerson, M., Aujean, M., Catinat, M., Goybet P. and Jacquemin A. (1988) *The Economics of 1992*, OUP, Oxford.

Emerson, M., Gros, C., Italianer A., Pisani-Ferry J. and Reichenbach H. (1992) *One Market, One Money*, OUP, Oxford.

Engel, C. and Rogers, J. H. (1996, December) 'How wide is the border?', *American Economic Review*.

European Commission (1990, October) 'One Market, One Money', *European Economy*, No. 44, Luxembourg.

European Commission (1998) *Infeuro Newsletter*, No. 8.

Fatas, A. (1998, April) 'Does EMU need a fiscal federation?', INSEAD Working Paper, *Economic Policy*, No. 26.

Fatas, A. (1997, January) 'EMU countries or regions? Lessons from the EMS experience', *European Economic Review*, Vol. 41.

Feldstein, M. (1977) *Foreign Affairs,* Vol. 76, No. 6, pages 60–73.

Flora, P., Kraus, F. and Pfenning, W. (1987) *State, Economy and Society in Western Europe, 1815–1975*, two volumes, London.

Forder, J. (1998a) 'The case for an independent European Central Bank: A reassessment of evidence and sources', *European Journal of Political Economy*, Vol. 14, pages 53–72.

Forder, J. (1998b) 'Central Bank Independence – Conceptual Clarifications and Interim Assessment', *Oxford Economic Papers*, Vol. 50, pages 307–34.

Forder, J. (1998c) 'Is the European Union really a Friend of Free Trade?', Politeia Lecture, 15 December 1998.

Friedman, M. (1968) 'The role of monetary policy', *American Economic Review*, pages 1–17.

Giavazzi, F. and Giovannini, A. (1989) *Limiting exchange rate flexibility: the European Monetary System*, MIT press, Cambridge, MA.

Gros, D. and Thygesen, N. (1991) *European Monetary Integration*, Longman, London.

Gros, D. and Thygesen, N. (1998) *European Monetary Integration: From the EMS to EMU*, London and New York.

Hummels, D., Rapoport, D. and Yi, Kei-Mu (1998, June) 'Vertical specialisation and the changing nature of world trade', *Economic Policy Review*, Vol. 4, No. 2, Federal Reserve Bank of New York.

IMF (1997, October) *World Economic Outlook*.

Johnson, C. (1996) *In with the Euro, out with the pound: the single currency for Britain*, London.

KPMG Management Consulting (1997) 'Europe's preparedness for EMU', Research Report.

Layard, R., Nickell, S. and Jackman, R. (1991) *Unemployment: macroeconomic performance and the labour market*, Oxford.

MacDougall, Sir D. (1992, May) 'Economic and Monetary Union and the European Community budget', *National Institute Economic Review*, National Institute of Economic and Social Research.

Mazower, M. (1998) *Dark Continent: Europe's twentieth century*, London.

Milesi, G. (1998) *Le Roman de l'Euro*, Paris.

Mundell, R. (1998, 24 March) 'Great Expectations for the Euro', *Wall Street Journal Europe*.

Nickell, S. (1997) 'Unemployment and Labour Market Rigidities: Europe versus North America', *Journal of Economic Perspectives*, Vol. 11, No. 3.

OECD (1994) *Country report on France*, Paris.

OECD (1995) *Country report on France*, Paris.

OECD (1997) *Country report on France*, Paris.

OECD (1998) *OECD Economic Outlook*.

Oppenheimer, P. and Forder J. (1996) 'The Changing Rationale of Monetary Union' in Hayward, J. (ed.) *Elitism, Populism and European Politics*, OUP, Oxford.

Padoa-Shioppa, T. (1994) *The Road to Monetary Union in Europe*, OUP, Oxford.

Pennant-Rea, R. *et al.* (1997) *The Ostrich and the EMU: policy choices facing the United Kingdom*, Centre for Economic Policy Research, London.

Porter, R. D. and Judson, R. A. (1996, October) 'The location of US currency: how much of it is abroad?', *Federal Reserve Bulletin*, Vol. 82.

Ramaswamy, R. and Sloek, T. (1997, December) 'The real effects of monetary policy in the European Union: what are the differences?', International Monetary Fund Working Paper WP/97/160.

Redwood, J. (1997) *Our currency, our country: the dangers of European Monetary Union*, London.

Sachs, J. and Sala-i-Martin, X. (1992) 'Fiscal Federalism and Optimum currency areas: evidence from Europe and the United States', in Canzoneri, M., Grilli, V. and Masson, P. (eds.) *Establishing a Central Bank: issues in Europe and lessons from the US*.

Samuelson, P. (1964, May) 'Theoretical notes on trade problems', *Review of Economics and Statistics*.

Szymanski, S. (1994, September) 'The City Labour market', in *The City Research Project*, Corporation of London.

Siedentop, L. (2000) *Democracy in Europe*.

Thygesen, N. (1998, May) 'EMU, Britain and other outsiders', Special Paper No. 102, Financial Markets Group, LSE.

Vinals, J. and Jimeno, J. F. 'Monetary Union and European Unemployment', Documento de Trabajo No. 9624, Servicio de Estudios, Banco de Espana.

Von Hagen, J. (1992) 'Fiscal Arrangements in a monetary union in Fair, S. and de Boissieu, C. (eds.) *Fiscal Policy, Taxes and the Financial System in an Increasingly Integrated Europe*, Kluwer, Dordrecht.

Index

BOTH SIDES OF THE COIN

THE ARGUMENTS FOR THE EURO

The euro was introduced in Euroland on 1 January 1999 and goes into everyday use on 1 January 2002. Will it usher in a new era of prosperity for Europe or will it precipitate financial disaster? What will be its effect on jobs? And on interest rates and mortgages?

The single currency fills the pages of the newspapers every day, but the arguments in favour of the euro are never set out clearly and concisely. Here, in an elegant essay by one of Britain's leading MEPs and economists, are the powerful arguments for joining the single currency. Christopher Huhne lucidly explains the arguments for the euro – cheaper capital, lower prices, more investment – and he shows why the disadvantages have been overstated.

Christopher Huhne makes the case for joining the euro persuasively and convincingly.

For the arguments against, turn this book over.

BOTH SIDES OF THE COIN

THE ARGUMENTS FOR THE EURO

by

Christopher Huhne

P

PROFILE BOOKS

First published in Great Britain in 1999 by
Profile Books Ltd
58A Hatton Garden
London EC1N 9LX
www.profilebooks.co.uk

This second edition published in 2001

1 3 5 7 9 10 8 6 4 2

Typeset in Galliard by MacGuru
info@macguru.org.uk
Printed and bound in Great Britain by
Bookmarque Ltd, Croydon, Surrey

A CIP catalogue record for this book is available from the British Library.

ISBN 1 86197 321 7

Contents

The author

Chris Huhne had two careers – as an economic and financial journalist, and as founder of one of the City's biggest teams of economists – before his third as a politician.

Now on the European Parliament's Economic and Monetary Affairs Committee that holds the European Central Bank to account, Mr Huhne was the draftsman for its first report on the ECB when he pressed for greater openness. Following that report, the ECB began to publish forecasts and its internal econometric models of the Euro-area.

Mr Huhne, Liberal Democrat MEP for South East England, is also the economic spokesman for the European Liberal Democrat and Reformist group. He recently chaired the expert commission on Britain's adoption of the Euro, and is a council member of Britain in Europe. He writes a weekly column on european affairs for the London *Evening Standard*.

Until 1999, Mr Huhne was group managing director of Fitch IBCA, an international debt rating agency. A former Council member of the Royal Economic Society, he has written three other economics books and articles for journals such as *Central Banking*, *The International Economy*, *Financial Stability Review* and the *Wall Street Journal*.

Until 1994, Mr Huhne was a columnist and business and city editor at the *Independent* and the *Independent on Sunday*. He worked for the *Guardian* for ten years as economics editor and columnist, and was Brussels correspondent of the *Economist*. In 1990, he won the Financial Journalist of the year award.

Preface and acknowledgements

This second edition is really another book, as we now have facts not just hypotheses. Eleven countries adopted the euro on 1 January 1999, and a twelfth – Greece – joined the euro group on 1 January 2001. So the euro has begun. All twelve countries will replace their national notes and coin with the new euro in the first part of 2002, and British holidaymakers will start to use euros for the first time that summer.

The debate about British membership will not go away. It is one of those defining issues which can reshape old loyalties. In this context, there has been a lot of low political debate that has largely used whatever projectiles happened to be at hand. But there has been too little elucidation of the real economic and political issues, although there could hardly be something more economic and political than the decision to adopt a new currency. We aim to fill the gap.

We have embarked upon the book in this form – in two halves, with a case for and a case against – to highlight the issues behind the decision. Although this is an argument, it is also designed to ensure that any intelligent reader of a British newspaper is able to cut through the chaff in the debate and focus on the important points. We have, however, imposed certain rules on ourselves. The data cited on each side in this book are not in dispute between us. What clearly differentiates us are matters of interpretation. How much weight should be given to one factor or another?

Every book of this kind owes a great debt to the others that have gone before. Thanks are also due to colleagues who directly or indirectly helped to shape some of these arguments. Chris Huhne particularly thanks Michael Emerson, with whom he wrote a previous book

on the single currency dealing with the general arguments applicable to Europe as a whole, Lillian Andenaes, whose research assistance in this second edition has been vital, and Sebastien Clerc-Renaud for statistical support. Chris would also like to thank specifically John Arrowsmith, Nick Clegg, Andrew Duff, Will Hutton, Richard Portes, Lionel Price, Vicky Pryce, Kitty Ussher and William Wallace for reading part or all of the manuscript in one or two editions and for helping to excise several errors of fact and interpretation. James Forder particularly thanks John Arrowsmith, Donna Bellingham, Ann Branch, Dominic Cumings, Andrew Haldenby, Allison Hoffman, Anand Menon, Malcolm Walter and Peter Oppenheimer. Those errors that remain are, of course, ours.

Christopher Huhne and James Forder
May 2001

1 **Introduction and summary**

Whether you are for the single currency or against it, you cannot doubt the importance of the issue for Britain. The single currency that eleven member countries adopted on 1 January 1999 is the most important development in Europe's economic history since the foundation of the common market in 1958. The euro is ushering in a golden age of European prosperity. It is creating a single economic space that reaches from Helsinki in the north-east to Cadiz in the south-west, and from Sligo in the north-west to Brindisi in the south-east. That area now encompasses not only the eleven founding members – France, Germany, Italy, Spain, Netherlands, Belgium, Luxembourg, Finland, Ireland, Austria and Portugal – but also Greece. The thirteen candidate democracies that will join the EU early in the new century, including Poland, Slovenia, Hungary, Estonia, Malta, Cyprus and the Czech Republic, are keen to adopt the euro. Can Britain really stand aside?

The euro, as an issue, has driven a meat cleaver through the Conservative Party and created doubters in the Labour Party and the Liberal Democrats too. It is one of those political issues that arrives once every two or three generations that has the capacity to divide former friends, and to remake tribal loyalties. The nearest parallels are Home Rule for the late-nineteenth-century Liberal Party, and the Repeal of the Corn Laws for the mid-nineteenth century Tories. It has been a long time since such a key issue has forced British politicians to put their judgement of the national interest ahead of their commitment to their party, right or wrong. As a result, this debate stirs passions like few others. But equally it tends to obscure the real economic arguments. Money, after all, is ultimately a convenience: a means of

exchange, a store of value and a unit of account. It is not a piece of national bunting to be waved like a flag. The idea that it should be a symbol is particularly bizarre, since the head of the British monarch did not appear on banknotes until 1960. (The Queen's head would continue to appear on coins if we joined the euro area.) Cutting through all the hype, the euro is just another word for money.

All the main British political parties are committed to holding a referendum before any decision to join, although in reality the Conservatives (with some notable exceptions such as former Chancellor Ken Clarke) want to defer a decision indefinitely. The Liberal Democrats' view is that we should make active preparations for membership, which would in turn help to resolve some of the remaining difficulties particularly with the high level of the pound. The Liberal Democrats' recent expert commission, which I chaired, advocated practical steps towards membership of a successful single currency at an appropriate exchange rate of €1.25 to €1.45 (or, in German mark terms, DEM2.45 to DEM2.84).[1]

The Labour government says that it is in favour of joining when the economic conditions are right. This is a reference to the five famous economic tests laid down by Chancellor of the Exchequer Gordon Brown in the Treasury report of October 1997.[2] Formally, the tests are to determine whether business cycles and economic structures are compatible, whether there is flexibility to deal with any problems, whether membership would encourage investment, whether it would help the City, and whether EMU would promote 'higher growth, stability and a lasting increase in jobs'. The principal objective of this part of this book is to persuade you that the answer to all those questions is yes. Those tests were set two years before the launch of the euro. Now that we have more than two years of experience with the currency, there is a lot of hard evidence to back up the claims for its beneficial effects. The euro is no longer an idea. It is a fact of life.

Britain's history in the European Union

Paul-Henri Spaak once said that there are two types of countries in Europe: those that are small and know it, and those that are small and do not. Britain has often fallen into the second category, and it is worth remembering some of our own history to see how Eurosceptic attitudes have led us astray in the past. British attitudes towards the European Community have, from the start, been marked by nothing but suspicion. The Messina talks of 1955 were to result in the Treaty of Rome of 1957, and the Common Market of the six original member states (France, Germany, Italy, Belgium, Luxembourg and the Netherlands). At those talks Whitehall took the view that the Treaty would have no chance of being agreed, ratified or applied; and if it were, it would be unacceptable to Britain. As we know, the outcome was different. The Treaty proved to be acceptable to Britain shortly afterwards.

There were very direct costs of that early episode of Euroscepticism which are relevant today, because we may be repeating the mistake with the euro. The first cost was that British business lost out from the trade liberalisation with all its new opportunities[3]. The second cost of Britain's Euroscepticism was just as severe. Many important policies were put in place without any consideration of British interests, since Britain was not a member. These proved to be a substantial burden when we had to accept them. The most onerous was the adoption by the original six of the Common Agricultural Policy's (CAP) high support prices, which were subsequently to involve a particular penalty for the UK as a large net food importer having to pay higher prices for food imports. The other big cost of being late was the Common Fisheries Policy (CFP), agreed in 1970. Neither the CAP nor the CFP would have been there if we had joined at the beginning.

Finally, we also joined the European Monetary System (EMS) – or exchange rate mechanism as it is called in the UK – in 1990, eleven years after it started. We missed the period from 1979 to 1983 when the exchange rates of the participants were realigned to make up for the

differences in their inflation rates. (If a country had an inflation rate 2 per cent higher than others, it would devalue its central exchange rate target, or 'parity', by 2 per cent to compensate).[4] In this period, the EMS was essentially designed to stop the financial markets' 'irrational exuberance'. We also missed the period from 1983 to 1987 when the fixed parities were moved to compensate for about half the difference in inflation, and the participants gradually squeezed inflation out of the system. And we joined, with a volatile exchange rate at a time of relatively high British inflation, when other countries were trying not to move their exchange rates at all and when the system was buffeted by the unique circumstances of German reunification.

As we shall see, there is a risk that the same tardiness in joining the single currency will involve similar costs. Once again, we have little influence over the early institutional arrangements for a system that, almost certainly, we will eventually join. Thus we had the embarrassing spectacle of a British Chancellor of the Exchequer – Gordon Brown – attempting to gatecrash the meetings of the euro group, the finance ministers of the founding eleven. Now that it is clear that the euro group has become the key body in discussions of economic and monetary policy, Mr Brown often fails to turn up to economic and finance ministers' meetings of the whole EU. When the world monetary authorities jointly intervened in the foreign exchange markets on 22 September 2000, the European Central Bank (ECB) mentioned only itself, the Bank of Japan and the US Federal Reserve. In effect, the world financial system is now run by the Group of Three – the United States, Japan and the euro area. The Bank of England had to put out a 'me, too' press release an hour or so later and was involved in only token intervention. If Britain were to declare its intention of joining the euro quickly, these political costs would be slight. But the longer we stay out, the more likely they are to mount. Outside the euro, we lose power, influence and sovereignty.

It is bizarre that British Eurosceptics try to argue that joining the euro would be like the ERM, because the euro was created in part as a

response to concerns that the ERM could not be sustainable. The objective of currency stability remained exactly the same, and for the same old reasons. If you do as much trade with your neighbours as most European countries, you cannot ignore your exchange rate because a drop adds so much to import prices and inflation, and a rise squeezes export prices and trade. But economic theory also told us that the exchange-rate mechanism was likely to come under severe strain, and this was predictable and predicted.[5] Theory suggested that you could have two out of three of the following objectives: fixed exchange rates, an independent interest-rate policy, and free capital flows. But having all three at the same time would be a felicitous accident. Once capital flows were liberalised, as they were in Britain in 1979 and in other member states like France as late as 1990, short-term money could flow to take advantage of higher interest rates. Either those interest rates would have to come down to a level consistent with the interest rates of the other pegged currencies, or other interest rates would have to go up. Or the exchange-rate link would have to be broken. Monetary union, a single currency, merely represents the decision to have free capital flows and a fixed exchange rate – with the sacrifice of an independent interest-rate policy for each country.

It is in this context that the frequent British jibe that 'they are only doing it for political reasons' should be seen. This is frankly absurd. Politics and economics are intimately entwined. Nothing of any consequence in economic policy is ever undertaken except for political reasons, and those political reasons may indeed be the promotion of prosperity for potential voters. Politicians who ignore the prosperity of their supporters are soon rejected. The single currency swam back on to the agenda in Europe in part because of the realisation that fixed exchange rates were unlikely to be sustainable, and because the alternative of free floating has traditionally been so disruptive. If EMU leads to a greater prosperity which in turn further binds together the member states of the European Union, is that an economic fact or a political one? Surely it is both, and both objectives are desirable. The

shared prosperity created by shared institutions to reconcile differences has kept the peace in Europe for longer than ever before in our continent's history.

The euro is here

For the 301 million people who live in the euro area, their national currencies are already fixed against each other. Their banknotes have merely become denominations of the underlying euro with fixed relationships (for example, €1=DEM1.956). They will be replaced by euro notes and coin in the first six months of 2002. People will soon be able to do business with nearly as few unnatural obstacles as exist within, say, the United States. Within the founding member states, as with all members of the European Union, people already have freedom of movement and freedom to work in each other's countries. They already have freedom to buy and sell goods, services and investments in other member states. But those freedoms have been inhibited because of the existence of different currencies. The cost of making a small cross-border payment can be prohibitive. And a sudden lurch in an exchange rate – for example, the jump of just 15 per cent in the Japanese yen against the US dollar in just a few days in early October 1998 – can wipe out planned profits on an export sale or an overseas investment.

But in a stable environment European businesses are able to deal with each other without worrying about a different currency. They can focus on what matters in their business relationships: is this purchase good value, and can I make a profit on this sale? The difficulties and risks of transactions that involve more than one currency are removed. As a result, there is more business being done. And more business means more investment, more prosperity and more jobs. As I will describe in detail later, the euro area grew in 2000 at its fastest rate for ten years. Jobs growth has been higher than in the United States or Britain since the launch of the euro, and business investment was the fastest growing element of all the different types of spending. The euro is bringing a new dynamism to Europe.

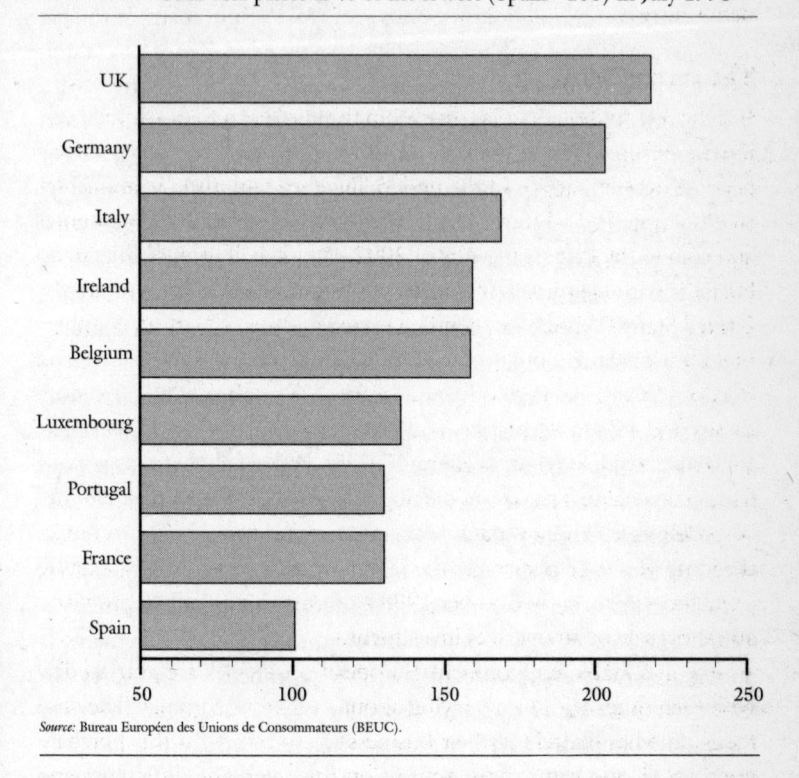

Figure 1.1   **Price differences: the real thing**
Coca-cola prices as % of the lowest (Spain=100) in July 1998

Source: Bureau Européen des Unions de Consommateurs (BEUC).

Even though the euro area's old national currencies will not be replaced until early 2002, there are increasing benefits for consumers. Before the euro, companies often charged widely varying prices, depending on what each national market will bear. A comparison of the cost of a Coca-cola bottle in July 1998 is shown in the chart: the price in Britain was more than double the price in Spain. However, companies are recognising that they will no longer be able to charge such varying prices without alienating their customers. It will simply

be too easy for consumers to compare prices, and shop around. From 2002, companies will need broadly the same prices (after allowing for transport costs) throughout the euro area. As a result, many of the big multi-nationals such as Unilever, Gillette and Astra-Zeneca are aligning their price lists. Some hope that they will be able to get away with an average of their old prices, but this is unlikely. The competitive characteristics of the big market are more likely to look like those of the more competitive national markets today: if a company tries to raise its prices in a particularly competitive national market, it soon finds itself undercut and losing business. The same will happen in the euro area as a whole. So highly priced euro area countries will tend to find the prices of traded goods move towards those in lowly priced countries.

This process is adding to the downwards pressure on prices from the gradual introduction of e-commerce (particularly in allowing businesses to put more of their components out to competitive tender) and from the gradual liberalisation of many markets within the European Union (that is, telecoms, electricity supply, gas). That in turn is causing businesses to search for new ways of cutting costs, and this is one of the factors behind the enormous surge in mergers and acquisitions in Europe. Scale helps businesses share development and information technology costs as well as other fixed overheads. The urge to merge is thus a natural consequence of increased competitive pressures. In 1999, the first year of the euro, the value of merger targets in which European companies were involved reached nearly $1.558 trillion, six times the level at the peak of the previous European mergers boom in 1990.[6] This very high rate of mergers continued at almost the same pace in 2000. Many of these mergers, including those in non-euro countries, were designed to prepare the merged entity for the challenges of the euro area.

Of course not all of this restructuring is due to the euro: there is a merger boom in the United States too. Mergers tend historically to go in waves, and often accompany peaks in the stock market. But the European merger boom has happened more rapidly than the boom in

Figure 1.2 **European mergers**
USD value of targets, millions

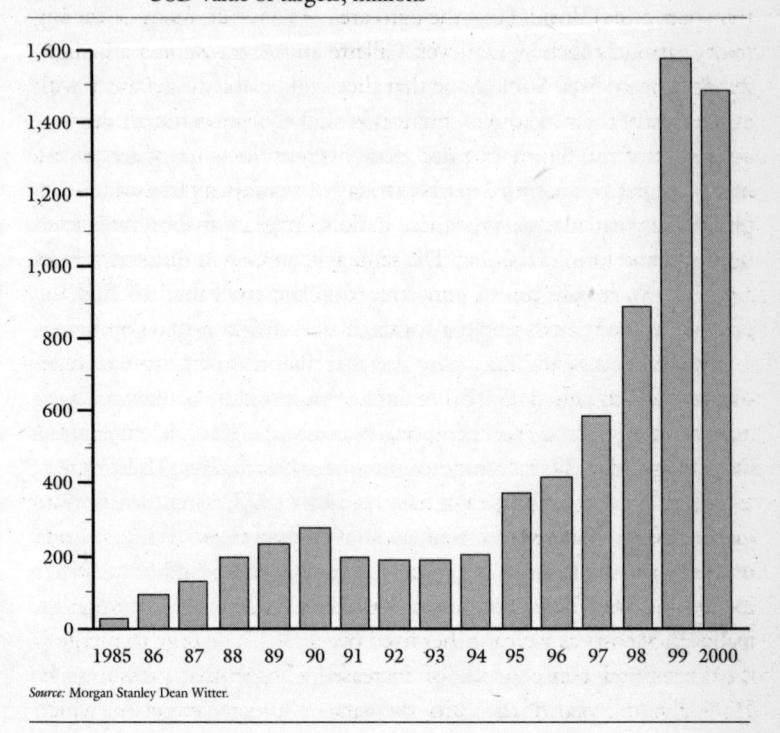

Source: Morgan Stanley Dean Witter.

the United States even though the stock market valuations have not been as enthusiastic. The value of merger targets within Europe rose 227 per cent between 1997 and 1999 against an equivalent rise of 84 per cent in the USA. There are also sound reasons for expecting that the European merger boom will go on for longer given the impact of the euro.[7] After all, Europe generally still has more businesses in any given sector of the market than the United States: for example, there are seven European car-makers against three in the United States, and twelve makers of railway engines against two in the United States.

Objectively, there is more room for consolidation in Europe, and the euro is a key factor in pressing for that change.

There is a twofold danger if Britain does not participate in the currency change that is spurring these developments. Some of Britain's biggest businesses – Unilever, Vodafone after its successful bid for Mannesmann, for example – may effectively come to regard the euro area as their real 'home' because that is where the largest part of their revenues and production operations is. For these businesses, their UK operations may increasingly come to be seen as a part of European or global operations. If the pound swings around violently, they will have an incentive to shift reporting, production and costs into the euro.

The second danger will be for small and medium-sized businesses based only in the UK. They may find that their competitors in the euro area are facing new competition, and are responding to that competition by merging and producing on a bigger scale. If so, they will find it increasingly difficult to compete even in the UK market. There may be a parallel here with the period from 1958 to 1973, when British businesses were sheltered from the extra competition of the original market-opening moves of the six founding EU members. When Britain eventually had to adjust to the new realities in the seventies, the pain was far worse as a result.

What of the sharp decline in the external value of the euro against the dollar, down at one stage by more than 30 per cent from its starting rate of €1 equals $1.17? In Britain's Eurosceptic press, this has been presented as dire news for the euro. But the only sensible objective for a big currency like the euro is internal stability, not its external value. After all, currencies have swung enormously since the breakdown of the Bretton Woods system in 1981. The pound fell from $2.40 in 1980 to $1.01 in 1985, and then bounced back sharply again over the next two years. A similar pattern affected the predecessor currencies of the euro: if they are weighted to create a 'synthetic' euro, the value of the currency was as high as $1.70 in December 1979 and as low as 69 cents in February 1985.[8] By 1987, the dollar was again so

weak that there had to be an international operation to rescue it. So large swings in exchange rates are nothing new. Such 'overshooting' has been a repeated feature of the foreign exchange markets and are very difficult for exporters to deal with given profit margins traditionally worth 10–20 per cent of the invoice.

Some overexcitable Eurosceptics have rather foolishly predicted that the fall in the euro's value against the dollar shows that the currency is doomed. However, these tend to be the same people who previously predicted that the single currency would never happen, and they ignore the evidence from the financial markets themselves. For example, the bond markets would extract a risk premium from weak euro area governments – say, the Italian or Belgian governments with much higher public debt to GDP ratios than the average – if investors thought that there was a serious risk of break-up in the euro area. But even the Italian government is able to borrow money from the financial markets at interest rates over a ten-year period which are lower than those in the United States. This is remarkable given that the Italian public debt to GDP ratio is double that of the United States.[9] Far from signifying a general loss of confidence in the euro, the external weakness of the euro against the dollar was simply another example of classic exchange-rate overshooting.

An important motive for the creation of the euro is to protect the euro area economies from the effects of those massive – and frequent – currency swings. In fact, the fall in the value of the euro against the dollar paradoxically underlines the new internal stability delivered by the euro. Precisely because so much trade is now internal to the euro area, and is therefore not affected by movements in exchange rates, the slide has had relatively modest effects. Import prices are up, and inflation has risen, but only to a peak of 2.9 per cent in the autumn of 2000, lower than the rate in the United States. Growth in the euro area in 2000, the second year of the new currency, was the highest for a decade, exceeding Britain's growth for the second successive year. Jobs growth in the leading euro area economies was also the highest for a

decade. Employment has been growing more rapidly in the euro area than in either Britain or the United States. Overall, more than 4.7 million net new jobs have been created in the first two years of the euro's existence,[10] and unemployment has fallen sharply. Given that the euro area has suffered two large external shocks – both the fall in the euro itself against the dollar, and the rise of oil prices – this is a surprisingly benign performance. It is hard to imagine any other European economic arrangements, certainly not free-floating exchange rates, or fixed exchange rates like the old exchange-rate mechanism, that could have delivered such a relatively positive outcome when faced with such challenges.

One comparison that highlights the beneficial impact of the euro is between Norway and Finland. In the run-up to the beginning of the euro system, it was noticeable how smooth the entry was for euro currencies that would previously have been buffeted by the commodity-price movements that occurred after the 1997 Asia crisis. For example, the Finnish mark glided smoothly into the euro area. By contrast, Norway, another commodity exporter, had a much worse experience. It had to hike interest rates seven times by a total of 4.5 percentage points to protect the crown, but even that served only to limit the fall in the crown to 7 per cent between the beginning of 1998 and October 1998. That defence of the crown, crucial to stop the explosion of import prices and inflation, weighed heavily on businesses and jobs – a familiar story to people in Britain who remember sterling crises of old.

Britain, too, has suffered from instability but in a different way. Sterling was bid up and up by the financial markets as our interest rates were put up to control domestic demand. From a low average of 2.26 German marks in 1995, sterling reached a peak of 3.46 German marks in May 2000, far above any estimate of its long-run sustainable value. As the graphic shows, sterling unit labour costs have risen sharply relative to our trading partners as a result of the rise of the pound. Indeed, the resulting rise in the pound (and therefore loss of competitiveness) was more severe during 1999 on most measures than it was

Figure 1.3   **Sterling real exchange rate (against euro zone) on the basis of unit labour costs in the whole economy (1980–97 = 100)**

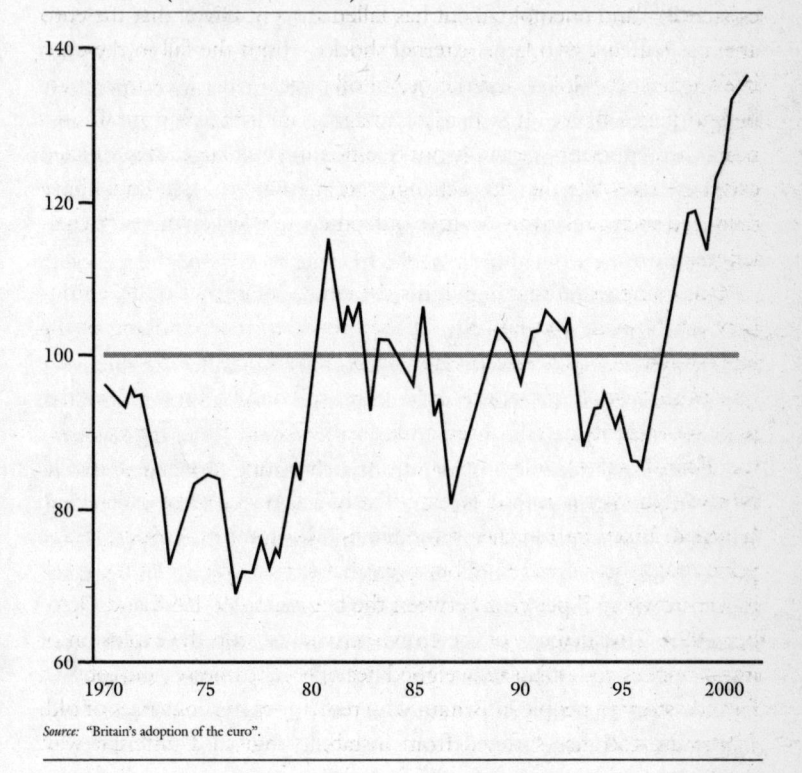

Source: "Britain's adoption of the euro".

even at the beginning of the 1980s (though British businesses are in a far better state to withstand such pressure). Remember that a typical profit margin on a business sale is somewhere between 10 and 20 per cent. That margin could be wiped out by this scale of currency change. How can our businesses plan their exports or their overseas investments with that sort of volatility?

The rise in sterling between 1995 and 2000 damaged Britain's

exporters by pricing them out of world markets. Nearly 350,000 jobs in manufacturing have been cut in little more than two years from March 1998 to September 2000. The list of major employers who cut back, often closing whole plants, includes some of the grandest names in business: General Motors, Ford, Corus (formerly British Steel), Matsushita, Nissan and so on. Overall manufacturing investment fell by a fifth in real terms from its 1998 peak to its low in 1999, and remained in 2000 some 15 per cent below the 1998 level. The number of businesses in Britain dropped by 4,700 in 1999. Many of these businesses and jobs would have been perfectly sustainable if the exchange rate against the euro had been stable. In other words, the independent existence of sterling has served to communicate a large shock to the trading sectors of the economy.

Far from acting as a useful policy lever that can influence the overall performance of the economy for the better – the central if unstated assumption of those who want to keep the pound – sterling has performed its usual role of being inappropriately strong or inappropriately weak. In the recent period, sterling has behaved more like a wrecking ball. Indeed, the episode is uncannily reminiscent of the overvaluation of 1979–81, which was duly succeeded by an opposite and equally inappropriate undervaluation. Outside the euro, there is every reason to suppose that the one word that will be most associated with 'sterling' is 'crisis'. All of this would be avoided if we adopted the euro.

To see the adoption of the euro, as the Eurosceptics do, as an evident matter of losing national sovereignty is simplistic and old-fashioned. The amount of national control afforded by a separate exchange rate and interest rate is far smaller than it was. Increasing global capital flows constrain national decision-making tightly, and those flows will often act irrationally. There have been long periods of over- and under-shooting in floating exchange rates. And the scale of those flows means that fixed but adjustable exchange-rate systems, like the European Monetary System that largely broke down in 1992, are no longer sustainable. So the euro is merely another way in which European

countries can re-exert some control over their monetary environment that they have otherwise largely lost. The choice is free floating – with frequent periods of shocks and misalignments – or the euro.

There is a parallel here between the euro and, say, legislation on environmental hazards, EU-wide industrial standards or consumer protection. If we want to control the sulphur emissions raining down on us, we need the Spanish and the French to control their emissions. If we want to sell our goods throughout a market of 375 million people, we need more than a 'free trade area': we need an agreement on common industrial standards of safety and consumer protection. Otherwise, each national market will block imports that do not comply with their own standards. In both cases, and in the case of the euro, national governments are no longer able to achieve what they want for their citizens without a European framework. Clean air, safe sea-water, protection against fraud in cross-border banking, the control of international crime – and monetary sovereignty – are all now objectives that need to be met by a government that reaches further than national boundaries.

The euro does not mean a superstate

People and politicians who are in favour of monetary union may also be in favour of greater political integration in Europe, but Chapter 5 will argue that there is no necessary connection between the two. There is no hidden agenda. Eurosceptics frequently argue that because former Chancellor Kohl or former President Mitterrand were in favour of monetary union as a means to greater political union, this is proof that it must be so. But people can be in favour of things for all sorts of reasons, and this does not make them right. Ideas and arguments should be assessed on their merits; not because you agree or disagree with the motivations of the people putting them forward.

In fact, there are many examples of monetary unions without political unions; such as Luxembourg and Belgium since 1921. to 1979, Ireland was in a monetary union with Britain,

one would argue that this either undermined the Irish national identity or led to political union. Indeed, President Eamon de Valera redrafted the Irish constitution to stress the differences with the United Kingdom, but the monetary link continued. And he exercised ultimate sovereignty by remaining neutral when Britain was at war, but the monetary union continued. The Maastricht framework for monetary union is similarly minimalist, but it stands a good chance of working without substantial amendment. And if it needs amendment, there will be a choice between devolving more power and responsibility to the participating states or to the common institutions in Brussels. It will not be a foregone conclusion, and it will not necessarily involve centralising more power at the centre of a superstate.

Indeed, the debate in the run-up to the negotiation on the new Treaty of Nice shows clearly how little appetite there is for any such superstate. First, the existing European institutions remain a small part of the totality of Europe's public sectors, with a budget accounting for 1.1 per cent of GDP in 2000 compared with 46 per cent of GDP spent by all levels of government. The Commission employs 23,000 people, fewer than half the number of Birmingham City Council with 56,000 staff. Secondly, the outstanding total of legislation at the European level has remained surprisingly static over the last ten years. True, there was an increase in EU law in the late 1980s to establish the single market (with common safety measures and standards). But the twin legislative chambers, the EU Council of Ministers and the European Parliament, have repealed as much as they have put on the statute book since that time. Thirdly, the member states that have been the greatest motors of integration – France and Germany – are hesitant in pressing for more. It is a paradox, given the German rhetoric in favour of political union, that Germany blocked an extension of majority voting in the Amsterdam intergovernmental conference, and that France had more objections to new areas of majority voting than any other member state in the Nice intergovernmental conference. To even the most hardened

Eurosceptic, the Nice summit and treaty were surely proof that the nation states remain in Europe's driving seat.

A European superstate, indeed, looks friendless. In President Jacques Chirac's formulation, there should be no united states of Europe, but a united Europe of states. Germany now wants a final treaty in 2004 to draw the limits to the European level of government, abandoning the commitment to 'ever closer union'.

The real point is not whether Britain will lose sovereignty by giving up the pound, but whether we will gain some control over our economic environment that we would not otherwise have. Sovereignty is to be used to secure our national interests; it is not some iconic figure to be placed in a glass case with a 'Do not touch' notice on it. We know this instinctively in the context of defence. We pool our sovereignty within the North Atlantic Treaty Organisation, and we give foreign generals the command of our men in matters of life and death. What greater sacrifice of sovereignty could there be? But we judge it to be worthwhile because it buys us security.

In the economic arena, we want stability, and the euro is the best way to achieve it. We want trade, prosperity, jobs and growth, and the euro can help us deliver all these. We want stable interest rates and more investment. And the euro will oblige. Or we can maintain the pound and luxuriate in a sovereignty which serves only as a delusion and a snare, turning our currency into another sad monument to the short-sightedness with which we have approached Europe for so long. We can have real power within Europe, or impotence outside.

2 **The advantages of the euro**

↓ UK & all Ezone

This chapter sets out the advantages of the euro for Britain along with all the countries that participate, before turning to some advantages purely specific to Britain.

The euro is a very simple change: one currency replaces twelve national ones. But this event in itself entails a whole series of economic consequences, the full nature of which becomes clear only on careful analysis. Much of the attention given to EMU concerns how it would affect the big decisions in the economy, such as interest rates and exchange rates. These macroeconomic effects are, of course, important. But critics of EMU tend to forget that its really important effects are likely to be on the small decisions made by thousands of individual companies. The real significance of EMU is that it makes markets work better.

Summary

EMU works in two fundamental ways. First, there are potential efficiency gains, such as the savings on the costs of exchanging one currency for another, and their likely effects on growth. Secondly, there are the gains that can be expected from reducing risks, such as the risk that your investment or export order will be made unprofitable by an exchange-rate change. These reductions in risk also encourage trade, investment and growth.

Efficiency gains

Lower transaction costs

An important, but, as we shall see fairly mundane, advantage of the euro is that it cuts the costs of transferring money from one country to another. These transactions costs have been highlighted in the example of the tourist who travels through each European country in turn

exchanging their original £100 for each successive currency. By the time they return to the UK, without spending anything except the commission on exchange transfers, they would have only £53 left.[11] The remainder would have gone on exchange commission.

Of course, no one in the real world would ever be put in such a position, but the example at least highlights the substantial costs of the process which afflict every tourist and every business involved in exports or imports. Transaction costs – the commission charges and artificially unfavourable exchange rates which banks use in buying or selling foreign currencies – are worth about 0.4 per cent of Gross Domestic Product (national income) in the European Union according to the surveys undertaken by the Commission.[12] Since this is an average, the figure is likely to be lower for Britain, because bigger countries do less trade than smaller ones. It may be no more than 0.2 per cent of GDP each year. Some have argued that this is insignificant, but every improvement counts. Moreover, these transaction costs weigh particularly heavily on small transactions, which can become prohibitively expensive. This may be one reason why such apparently small costs may have a sizeable impact in deterring trade, as we shall see.

Easier price comparisons

In terms of efficiency, a key advantage of EMU is in making prices easy to compare. Many businesses are using price tags showing both the national currency and euros. But once those national notes and coin are replaced by euro notes and coin – a process taking place in the first few weeks of 2002 – another important economic effect will come fully into play. Very quickly, consumers will be able to compare prices easily across national markets. New competitive forces will be unleashed bringing new efficiency gains.

For small items that do not cost much, this new competition is unlikely to matter. But for big-ticket consumer durables, ranging from cars to washing machines and televisions this new ease of price

comparisons (so-called price 'transparency') is likely to have dramatic effects. Consumers, wholesalers and traders will naturally buy from the cheapest source, and in so doing they will put enormous pressure on companies to reduce prices and to increase their competitiveness. If a company tries to rig the market by charging higher prices in one part of the euro area, traders will soon start buying their goods in the cheaper parts and selling them in the more expensive ones. Price differences will become steadily less sustainable. This undercutting will benefit efficient producers, who will be able to take greater advantage of economies of scale. This ease of comparison is already scaring lots of big companies into producing new price lists which, for the first time, are the same throughout Europe. Multinationals will no longer be able to hide behind the veil of national currencies.

In the Introduction, I cited the case of Coca-cola. Another example of where this effect may be important is the car market, where for many years substantial national price differences have continued despite the best efforts of the Commission and national competition authorities to reduce them. This is almost certainly due to anti-competitive restraints on trade, but the manufacturers justify the differences by blaming exchange rates. That will no longer be possible in EMU.

The full significance of these price differences was dramatically illustrated in a recent study of the United States and Canada[13]. This looked at prices for products on each side of the US–Canadian border (and therefore each side of the currency divide between the US and Canadian dollars). If the market worked properly, then changes in prices in one city would be mirrored quickly by changes in prices in another. This is a reasonable test of the so-called 'law of one price'. But the study discovered that the border allowed prices for the same products to differ by a large amount; indeed, the cross-border price differences were equivalent to those created by vast distances within a single market, with all the transport costs involved. Similar price differences for the same products within the United States and Canada occurred

Table 2.1 **Price comparisons for popular cars in EU countries, 2000**

Car model	Cars sold in 1999	Tax free price in UK	Cheapest country	UK price as % of cheapest
Ford Focus	103,228	£8879	Denmark	165.1
Ford Fiesta	99,830	£6318	Denmark	151.5
Vauxhall Astra	92,050	£10,034	Denmark	170.0
Vauxhall Corsa	86,779	£6379	Greece	151.4
Vauxhall Vectra	77,479	£12,000	Denmark	175.0

Source: EU Commission Competition Directorate-General

only at a distance of 1,780 miles. So borders introduced substantial hurdles to traders despite a lack of trade barriers and (mainly) a common language.[14]

Given that there are far more borders in Europe, the conclusion has to be that EMU will benefit consumers even more. It could, indeed, have similar effects to some of the great technological advances that dramatically reduced transport costs, increased consumer choice and raised living standards. An example would be the introduction of the steamship on the North Atlantic in the late nineteenth century, which slashed the cost of shipping grain from the US Midwest to Europe, and threw up enormous new business opportunities in both continents. EMU is a way of shrinking Europe, and bringing competing businesses far closer together to the great benefit of their customers.

Cheaper finance for businesses

The persistence of substantial price differentials is not confined to manufactured items. It also applies to some crucial services that have an important knock-on effect on the efficiency of other businesses, particularly banking. Indeed, some of the most exciting effects of EMU are

on this key sector, which moves people's savings into the most efficient investment uses. The euro is creating cheaper finance for many companies, and opening up whole new sources of risk capital for businesses that until now have been unable to raise money. The effect is to make the European economy much more dynamic.

Different currencies matter more in banking and finance than almost anywhere else, precisely because money is the raw material of the banking world. This is why there has been limited progress in creating a financial 'single market' until the advent of the euro. The Commission's own studies of the price divergences within member states for standard banking products shows that they actually increased since the launch of the single market. Clearly, the existence of loyal customer bases locked in separate national currencies has allowed some banks to raise charges disproportionately. The single market, on its own, had minimal effects in this key industry; only a single currency can make the single market a reality.

After EMU, there is nowhere to hide. Banks have to become more efficient, reducing costs to compete in passing on the benefits to their customers. The process of consolidation has already begun: the Dutch bank ING has recently bought Belgium's Banque Bruxelles Lambert; Nordbanken of Sweden has merged with Merita of Finland; Belgium's Generale Bank merged with Fortis of the Netherlands. In Germany and Italy domestic mergers may still have a way to run since there are a lot of banks. Germany's Deutsche Bank has tried two domestic merger bids – with Commerzbank and Dresdner – which failed in the detailed negotiations.

This process of increased competition and consolidation among banks will particularly benefit small and medium sized businesses, which are the customers most likely to shop around. Moreover, these businesses will also begin to benefit from another source of finance: the markets for shares and bonds. EMU has added to the pressures for the integration of European stock exchanges. Investors are now less interested in comparing Italian and German market levels, than in comparing

pharmaceutical companies or engineering companies wherever they are based in the euro area. The comparison is less national and more sectoral. As the shareholder culture takes root, it is becoming easier for companies focused on delivering shareholder value (in terms of increased dividends and capital gains) to raise new equity capital when they need it. This new shareholder culture fomented by EMU will also be a source of pressure on companies to become more efficient and profitable.

The bond market – the market in securities that pay an interest rate, as opposed to equity securities whose dividends vary with profits – is also becoming a potent source of new finance. The buyers of most bonds are naturally conservative. They want an assured return, and they look overwhelmingly to bonds issued in their own currencies. Many of them, particularly insurance companies and pension funds, have explicit rules which ensure that their assets (shares, bonds and so forth) are mainly in the same currency as their liabilities (the future pay-outs of insurance claims or pensions). In the past, this constrained them to invest in their own national markets. Since those were small, it was often not possible to put together portfolios that would spread risks. So they were driven to hold risk-free government bonds.

Since 1 January 1999 Europe's institutional investors have been able to buy any securities in the euro area and still preserve their conservative policy of matching the assets and liabilities in their home currency. The ability to put together larger portfolios of bonds means that they are able to reduce the risk of holding individual securities. In other words, investors can spread their eggs over more than one basket, reducing the risk of a problem. And that in turn means that they can afford to buy bonds that are individually riskier, even though the portfolio as a whole may be less risky.

The result? EMU has caused an explosion in the European corporate bond market, as the graphic shows. New corporate bond issues quintupled between 1998 and 1999. Within the resurgent corporate market, there is a shift towards riskier securities: the more lowly rated securities (rated BBB and below) accounted for 9.6 per cent of new

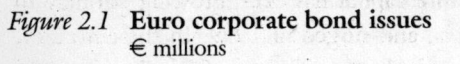

Figure 2.1   **Euro corporate bond issues**
€ millions

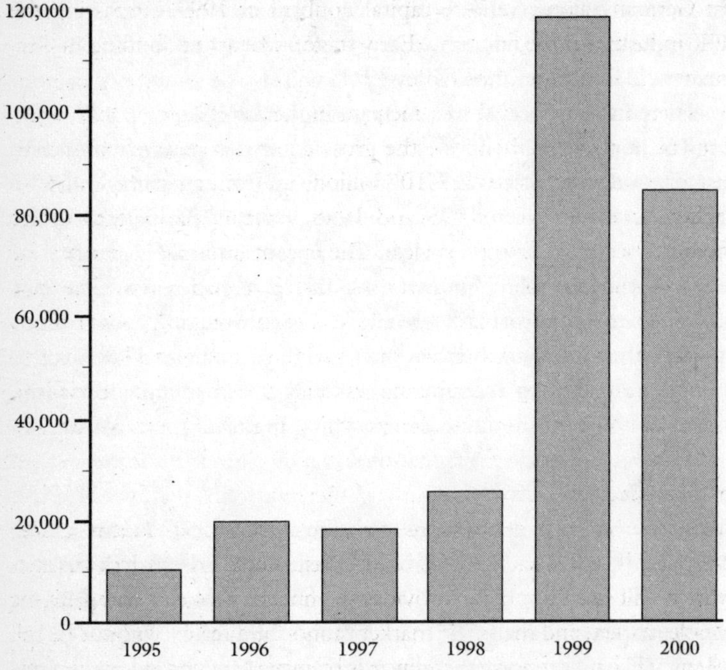

Source: Fitch Ratings.

bonds in 1996 but this had risen to 18.4 per cent in 1999.[15] The European high yield market – what the Americans impolitely call 'junk bonds' – has been born too, helping to raise finance for much riskier ventures. European investors are coming to resemble their American counter-parts: Europe's traditional dislike of risk was not an inherent cultural trait, but an artificial result of the multiplicity of currencies.

A similar phenomenon has also begun to occur in the equity markets. There is much more finance available for early start-ups and for

expanding businesses: venture capital has been growing strongly in Europe since the mid-1990s, and surged in 1999. In the euro area, total venture capital funding rose by 84 per cent to €7 trillion in 1999. In Germany alone, venture capital doubled in 1999, surpassing the UK industry for the first time. Early stage and start-up funding in Germany was four times the UK level.[16]

There has also been a vast increase in the appetite for public offerings of new shares. In 1999, the gross equity issuance of companies listed in the euro area was €107 billion, up from an average of €56 billion a year between 1995 and 1998. Overall, the pattern in the financial sector in Europe is clear. The end of multiple currencies, by encouraging portfolios, is increasing the appetite for risk. The new scale and ease of use of the euro markets is encouraging companies to go directly to investors rather than use the banking middle-man to raise money. And by encouraging risk-taking and entrepreneurialism, the euro is also encouraging the growth potential of the euro area.

Some gains, some losses

These are some of the reasons why the most crucial benefit arising from the single currency will be the vast, new and efficient markets which will open up. EMU provides the final keystone to complete the single market, and the single market cannot be a reality without EMU. Many will gain extraordinary rewards by providing new goods and services on a greater scale at a far cheaper price. But some are right to fear the outcome. The environment is bound to become more competitive. Some will lose and go to the wall. There will be some job losses, even if overall there are gains. But such costs will not last long.

Indeed, the effort to create a real single market in the late 1980s was widely expected to lead to job losses before it brought benefits. The opposite happened. Businesses anticipated the effects by increasing their investment. The result was an investment boom and an overall fall in unemployment. Though some people lost their jobs more new jobs were created so that there was a net rise overall. Most crucially,

however, economists know of no other way in which long-run prosperity can be increased other than through productivity and efficiency improvements of the sort that EMU should encourage. The important concern is not to protect specific jobs, but to ensure that the economy is dynamic and can create new ones. If we did not encourage such changes, we would still be taking the stagecoach to Bath and asking an ostler to rub down the horses. Every month the economy loses hundreds of thousands of jobs; the important objective is to ensure that it creates just as many or more than it loses. The only constant in economic life is change.

How far reaching will these changes be? In traditional economic theory these gains from greater competition and market efficiency ought to be a one-off improvement in the way of doing things, even if they are spread over a number of years. In reality, though, such a one-off improvement in efficiency may have more lasting effects. They may become, in the jargon, 'dynamic' gains. The most important point is that more output can be produced with a given amount of capital investment. That in turn means that capital investment becomes more attractive to businesses because the returns on capital have increased. Capital investment will therefore rise.[17]

There is another reason to expect that the market-widening and market-deepening impact of monetary union might improve growth. Traditional economic theory about growth assumes that it comes about because of technological innovation and that there are diminishing returns to investment (that is the more you do, the less you get back for each extra amount of investment). But the new growth theories point out that there may be increasing returns to investment for many businesses at many times. In other words, the extra profit on extra investment actually goes up. This happens, for example, because of constant overhead costs (such as investment in computer programmes) which would be a diminishing part of any increased output and sales. If this is so, the growth impact of the single market, completed by monetary union, could be more substantial. It will allow

European producers to reap substantial extra returns by producing on an altogether larger scale than they have done in the past.

Reducing risks

Less exchange-rate uncertainty: more trade and more investment

So far, we have discussed the reasons for expecting higher growth due to efficiency gains. But there is another set of reasons too: we may get higher growth due to less risk.

The replacement of national currencies immediately reassures everyone involved in foreign trade or investment with our European partners that they will no longer suffer sudden losses because of exchange-rate shifts. This is surprisingly significant: even for countries participating in the exchange-rate mechanism the monthly variability of the exchange rate had been more than 0.5 per cent up or down. For countries outside, such as Britain, the monthly variability has been nearly 2 per cent.[18] In other words, the random workings of the foreign exchange market may deprive a trader or an investor of that sort of difference. And remember that this margin is very large compared with typical profits of 10–20 per cent of the invoice.

This variability has reduced trade by generating uncertainty about the long-run level of the exchange rate, and is one reason why so many European businesses continually stress the importance of a stable exchange rate, quite apart from the level.[19] These risk-reducing effects were, until recently, highly conjectural. Economists generally were unable to find a large impact of exchange-rate uncertainty on trade flows. However, the conventional wisdom has now changed.

There is an increasing number of studies suggesting that currencies do affect trade. One study shows that a Canadian province trades twenty times more goods and services with another Canadian province than with an equidistant US state, and these startling results were subsequently supported in a second piece of research.[20] In other words, there is very strong 'home bias' in trade. Borders matter. Separate currencies are a serious obstacle.

Another study that looked at the surprisingly large number of monetary unions in the world today: 92 countries or territories are currently in some kind of official common currency scheme. It used a model to predict how much trade would normally be conducted between countries (largely based on their relative prosperity and their distance from each other) and then looked at whether monetary unions affected the outcome. It concluded that a country conducts three times as much trade with a country with which it shares a common currency as with other countries that are equidistant.[21] Surveys repeatedly show businesses themselves thoroughly dislike the uncertainties associated with exchange-rate movements. For example, a recent survey of European businesses employing more than 5,000 people found that 87 per cent of the companies expected to benefit from EMU, and that 58 per cent cited reduced exposure to currency fluctuations.[22] Why would they say such a thing if currency swings were not a source of concern?

We should therefore expect that British membership of the euro area would substantially increase trade with our most important market. But the abolition of such exchange-rate risks would also have financial consequences. As a result of currency uncertainty investors have often required an extra interest rate – a risk premium – on the securities of countries that are perceived to be at risk of devaluation. This was the case even when long-standing membership of the ERM had reduced actual variability (as in France, Belgium and the Netherlands for many years). This raises the real interest rate for everyone who borrows in that country, cutting off potential investment, jobs and growth.

Monetary union makes these interest rate costs vanish. It dramatically reduces the risk of investing in another country within the union. Therefore it also reduces the 'hurdle rate' or target rate of return which a business may require on its investment, and in so doing investment projects which were marginal before become possible under EMU. As a result, some investments will be undertaken which would not happen under present circumstances. Investment should rise, and the potential

growth rate of the euro area economy should increase. Most importantly, that growth and investment should also allow a sustainable fall in unemployment. EMU should mean more jobs overall, even if some individuals and companies will be adversely affected.

This point about increased investment sometimes surprises people, because in theory businesses can insure, or 'hedge', against exchange-rate risks. But the reality is that the forward and futures markets in foreign exchange are usually available for only a year or two ahead. That is enough to protect a trader, but even so the protection is imperfect and it costs money. Indeed, such an insurance policy can be a substantial part of any multinational's financial costs. Moreover, such an insurance policy does not stop the underlying problem from occurring: you get a pay-out, but the house has still burned down. If the company has become uncompetitive in producing particular goods, it will still be rational for the management to cut costs or production. The profit on the insurance policy may cushion the blow, but it will not avert the outcome. You cannot hedge (or insure against) costs. And there have been many examples of companies which have faced serious difficulties because of moves in exchange rates, including most of the manufacturing sector in 1979–81 and again in 1997–2000.

These hedging problems are compounded when we consider a business that is thinking of investing in another country, rather than just selling to its consumers. It is possible, of course, for a big business to borrow entirely to make the investment in the currency of the country in which it is investing. Then if the currency drops, the earnings flow and the value of the investment drop in terms of the company's home currency, but so does the liability (the borrowing) by an equivalent amount. This is a very good insurance against the uncertainty of the exchange rate. However, only the largest companies are credit-worthy enough to be able to borrow to fund overseas investment in this way (and even they rarely do so). More typically, companies are required by banks or by other lenders to put a substantial slice of equity finance into a subsidiary, and they may also lend money from head office to the

company. In these circumstances the company is clearly taking an exchange-rate risk.

By eliminating that risk such a company should be more willing to invest in other member states of the euro area. Business concepts that are successful in one member country can be 'rolled out' more rapidly into others. And these business concepts usually come from precisely those small and medium-sized businesses which are most affected by exchange-rate uncertainty today, and which are the most dynamic part of every economy. This is not a zero-sum game where one person wins what another person loses: a reduction in uncertainty will help everyone by boosting investment that would not be undertaken today. Investment will criss-cross the euro area, helping to revive areas that have fallen on hard times and where people offer their services relatively cheaply.

What sort of impact could this have? Baldwin argues that there could be a reduction in the amount that businesses expect to compensate for risk (the risk premium) of about 1 percentage point, but that a drop of half a percentage point is a reasonable central estimate. A reduction in the risk premium of just 0.5 per cent could lead to long run increases in productive capacity and eventually in output of between 5 and 10 per cent, which is a very significant figure.[23] Such an outcome will only become clear over time, but already the evidence from the euro area is consistent with the view that there will be major investment-boosting effects from the reduction of risk. Business investment is growing very rapidly in the euro area: indeed, investment for the last three years (1998 to 2000) grew at more than three times the 1981–96 average in each year.

For those with some knowledge of economic history, this will not come as a surprise. In the last period in which the world economy enjoyed genuinely fixed exchange rates (under the gold standard which lasted from 1880 until the outbreak of the First World War) the level of international investment was much greater than it is today. At that time there was no exchange-rate risk in investing in another country

Table 2.2 **Capital flows under the gold standard compared with recent years**

Current account balances as a percentage of GDP

Gold standard 1880–1913		Post-war 1965–1986	
Country	%	Country	%
Britain	4.5	Britain	0.0
Germany	1.8	Germany	0.9
Italy	0.6	United States	0.0
Sweden	−2.7	Japan	0.7
Norway	−2.5	France	0.2
Denmark	−2.6	Belgium	0.0
Australia	−3.7	Norway	−2.1
Canada*	−7.7	Canada	−1.5
Finland	−1.6		
Greece	−3.1		

*Average of data for 1900 and 1910

Source: Tamim Bayoumi, International Monetary Fund, 1989

since almost all countries were committed to exchanging their national currency for a fixed amount of gold (or a currency like sterling which was in turn linked to gold). Indeed, you could say that there was effectively a world monetary union. This meant that businesses could concentrate on the underlying risk of the investment without the worry and the false signals introduced by exchange-rate movements.

Table 2.2 shows the results. Capital flows as a percentage of national output (GDP) in the period from 1880 to 1913 were far higher than they are today. The average annual inflow into Australia over the entire period was nearly 4 per cent of GDP, nearly double the scale of flows in the period 1965 to 1986 to the largest recipient in the comparison. Canada was even more spectacular, recording nearly 8 per cent of GDP

inflows in each year, which is more than the amount in a single year which catalysed the Mexican crisis in December 1994 or the Thai crisis in July 1997.

Once again, the early evidence from the beginning of the euro area is that it is indeed facilitating much larger cross-border flows. The capital inflows into Portugal, for example, were worth more than 10 per cent of GDP during 2000, nearly three times the average annual inflows over the period 1981–1996. [24] Such an inflow, the exact counterpart of the current account of the balance of payments, may well have provoked a financial crisis in previous periods without the assurance of monetary union. Now investors can put money into Portugal without the old worry that devaluation would undermine the value of their investment. They will continue doing so until they believe that the higher potential returns in low income Portugal have been exhausted, and they will not be deterred by the risk of a sudden exchange-rate crisis. We will return to this point in more detail in the following section on balance of payments constraints.

Lower interest rates

This risk-reducing boost to investment may be augmented by a reduction in interest rates. If Britain joined, there may be some cut in interest rates, whether on borrowing linked to short term interest rates (such as most variable-rate mortgages) or borrowing at long maturities and fixed interest rates. At the end of November 2000, British short-term interest rates were 6 per cent against 5 per cent in Germany and in France. British ten-year interest rates (on government bonds) were almost exactly the same as those in Germany at 5 per cent. The cash effect for a £46,000 mortgage holder of a cut to German levels would be £460 a year, or £38 a month.[25] Corporate borrowers that issue bonds at longer maturities should also benefit from the larger and more liquid bond market that exists in the euro area.

Short-term interest rates, of course, move up and down according to the business cycle and policy decisions. However, there is some evi-

dence that interest rates in the UK are relatively high in real terms, after allowing for inflation, throughout the business cycle.[26] The risk of a fall in sterling may be an important explanation for the differences. Investors require higher interest rates to compensate for higher risks. Joining the monetary union might over time reduce the real interest rate in the UK, which would boost investment and growth.

If interest rates are lower, should pensioners be worried about their income? Not at all. Their savings would not be eroded by inflation as they have been so often in Britain in the last thirty years. Moreover, pensioners with savings in bonds and shares should see further capital gains as lower interest rates make them look more attractive. Borrowers benefit from lower interest costs, but savers benefit from greater security and from capital gains on other investments. EMU benefits both savers and investors.

Moreover, there should be another big benefit for both borrowers and lenders in the euro area: interest rates as a whole ought not just to be lower but also to be more stable. They will not be subject to the enormous swoops and surges that have bedevilled British interest rates over the last thirty years. The framework for monetary policy in the euro area guarantees that political gerrymandering ahead of elections cannot happen. The people who decide interest rates are politically disinterested central bankers. But that is also the case in Britain now that the Bank of England's Monetary Policy Committee sets interest rates. (We will turn to the political arguments on this issue in the chapter on the political consequences of EMU.) Indeed, every major economy now distances its politicians from day-to-day control of interest rates (although Britain, typically, was the last of the big seven industrial economies to make its central bank independent.)

But the likely stability of euro area interest rates is also an effect of averaging. The euro area is a big area where some parts will be expanding rapidly while others are growing slowly. Because interest rates will reflect average monetary conditions throughout the euro area, they will be more stable than interest rates that reflect the ups and downs of

the individual countries. Macroeconomic forecasters know this effect well from forecasting GDP (overall output) and its components (consumers' expenditure, investment and so forth). GDP is much more stable than the components.

Fewer balance of payments constraints

There is one other growth effect that could be important. In the past there has been some evidence that governments become worried if a large difference develops between the exports of goods and services, and the corresponding amount of imports. Such a current-account deficit on the balance of payments has to be financed by capital inflows, and a rapid reversal or just a cessation of those flows can cause an unpleasant crunch. This, indeed, is what happened in Asia in 1997 and 1998. The exchange rate weakens sharply or interest rates have to be raised sharply to hold the exchange rate. In this sense there may be a balance of payments constraint on growth because of the fear of the way in which the exchange market may react. By abolishing the internal exchange rate between EU member states, this constraint on policymakers is lifted. Each member country has equal access to the foreign exchange generated by the collectivity. Growth can continue at its natural rate without interruption by a stop–go cycle. For Britain, which has long been bedevilled by perceived balance of payments weakness and by sterling crises, this could be a particular boon.

The impact of the lifting of balance-of-payments constraints will become clear as the size of the capital flows, which must equal the size of the current account of the balance of payments, grows within Europe's monetary union. Although it is early days, the first evidence that EMU is lifting an important hurdle comes from Portugal. The Portuguese current-account deficit was 9 per cent of GDP in 1999, 10 per cent of GDP in 2000, and was set to widen further thereafter. By common consent this size of current-account deficit would, if Portugal still had a separate currency, have provoked a crisis with a run on the escudo. Indeed, such a crisis occurred on the last occasion that Portu-

gal ran a similar deficit worth 11.6 per cent of GDP in 1982. The escudo dropped by nearly 30 per cent in two years; the government slammed on the brakes so that domestic expenditure fell by 4.4 per cent in 1983 and 5.6 per cent in 1984; national output declined in 1983 and unemployment subsequently hit a new peak. By contrast, Portugal is now expected to register continued growth freed from balance-of-payments constraints by its EMU membership. Portuguese growth will eventually slow down as unused resources are entirely employed and wages rise to make investment less attractive. But EMU will have spurred Portugal's catch-up, and will have removed an important obstacle to growth.

How important are the efficiency and growth gains?

Putting numbers on these efficiency and growth gains is extremely tentative, not least because the nitty-gritty of improving the efficiency of markets is less easy to quantify than grand claims about the effects of a cut in interest rates or a boost in public spending. But the microeconomic effects matter, as the impact of trade liberalisation has shown. And it is clear that the orders of magnitude are likely to be substantial.

The EU Commission has estimated a growth bonus of 0.7 per cent a year[27] due to efficiency gains alone, disregarding the reduction in risks. The range could be anything from 0.4 per cent to 1 per cent a year, a substantial amount given that the underlying trend growth rate of the European economy is perhaps 2.5 to 3 per cent a year. However, it would be wrong to succumb to the numbers game. Many big changes in economics cannot be quantified, but are crucial nonetheless. How would one quantify, for example, the impact of the creation of the Bretton Woods institutions in stabilising the world economy? Yet few doubt that they were essential contributors to the post-war boom in the 1950s and 1960s.

An idea of what even small gains from EMU might mean can be gauged from the following calculation. Assume that the benefits are just 0.25 per cent extra growth a year, which has to be a very conservative

estimate. The wonders of compound interest mean that an extra quarter per cent growth a year, for someone on average (median) earnings of £18,346[28] in Britain, soon cumulates to a substantial benefit. At a trend growth rate for the economy as a whole of 2.1 per cent a year in real terms, this should have gone up to £22,584 in ten years' time (at today's prices). Add an EMU bonus of 0.25 per cent a year, and the figure would be £23,143, a real rise of £599 or 2.5 per cent. If it is double that, the real rise would be nearly £1,200. EMU is not like winning the national lottery, but it is not negligible either. Even the slowest increase would be the equivalent to more than an extra year's pay increase every ten years. And if the Commission is right, it will be the equivalent of an extra year's pay increase every three years.

Let me summarise these arguments about advantages. First, EMU is increasing efficiency. It is completing the single market. Businesses can exploit opportunities on a wider scale, and there will be substantial efficiency gains not just through a reduction in transaction costs but also through increasing returns to large investments. The rate of return will therefore increase. Second, EMU reduces risks. The monetary arrangements are creating new and more liquid markets where securities investors are more willing to take risks because they can spread them more widely. There is therefore an increase in the availability of capital and a reduction in its cost. In addition, the abolition of exchange-rate uncertainty will reduce the risks attaching to companies' fixed investment, and will therefore reduce the target rate of return that businesses seek. The reduction in the cost of capital, the cut in the target rate of return and the rise in the prospective rate of return, will all encourage investment. This will raise the trend growth rate of the European Union economies. EMU will make us richer, quicker.

None of these arguments are controversial. All that a critic can say is that each point is doubtful, and the effects may not be important. But that does not look credible when there are so many arguments about microeconomic gains all of which point in the same direction.

  it consistent with the early evidence of what is happening to

product, labour and financial markets in EMU. It also belies what we know of economic history and success: big, competitive markets breed more successful companies and higher living standards. The history of trade integration within the EU is testament to that. So is the success of the United States, which remains richer than any other comparable industrial country not because its monetary or fiscal policies have been pursued with greater dexterity – that is hardly the case – but because its continent-wide market has led to efficiency that no other country can emulate.

Other advantages

A new world currency

Apart from the growth and efficiency effects of the euro, there is also a more nebulous but potentially significant benefit in having a nascent world currency. First, the creation of Europe-wide deep and liquid capital markets, for both equities and debt securities, will gradually make those securities more attractive to people outside the euro area. Many official foreign-exchange reserve managers today, for example, hold a disproportionate amount of US government Treasury bills and bonds simply because of the attractive liquidity (the ease of buying and selling, even in bad times) of those New York markets. Asset managers have the assurance that they will always be able to get their money quickly if necessary. By contrast, European bond markets have been fragmented by national currencies, but are now becoming more liquid and attractive as the effects of currency segmentation wither. A portfolio shift towards euro-markets might reduce the cost of funds for business still further.

The table shows how the dollar has been disproportionately important as a world currency even though the European and the American economies are a similar size, and European exports are bigger than US exports. In the first year of the euro's launch, this began to shift with the euro becoming more popular as a currency in which to borrow. Although the table shows that fewer than a third of all outstanding

Table 2.3 **United States, Japan and the EU: Relative size, and use of currencies, %**

	USA	Japan	EU	Of which euro area
Share of world GDP, 1999	21.9	7.6	20.3	15.8
Share of world exports 1999 (ex EU or ex euro area in the case of EU-11)	16.0	10.0	19.0	19.0
Use of currencies in trade	48.0	5.0	31.0	n.a.
Use in international debt securities, % outstandings end 1999	47.0	10.0	n.a.	29.1
Use in developing country debt, % of outstandings, end 1999	72.4	8.2	n.a.	16.8
Denomination of global foreign-exchange reserves, 1999	66.2	5.1	16.5	12.5
Foreign-exchange transactions, 1998	43.5	10.5	31.5	26.0

Note: GDP is at purchasing power parities.

Source: Eurostat, EU Commission and IMF World Economic Outlook, October 1997

debt securities were denominated in euro or euro-legacy currencies at the end of 1999, this merely reflects the fact that it takes time for an annual flow to change a very large stock of debt. Some 47 per cent of net bond issues during the year took place in euros while the dollar share was 44.9 per cent. To the extent that the borrowers held and used their euros – selling them in the foreign exchange market – this new-found popularity for the euro helped to weaken the currency. What appears to have happened is that borrowers took advantage of the euro more rapidly than investors switched their portfolios into euros. As investors also begin to find the euro attractive, this will become a factor

in the recovery of its external value and in the reduction of its interest rates.

A challenge to the dollar?

A second effect of the euro is likely to be that many people outside Europe will want to hold euro banknotes as a means of exchange and a store of value. In time, the euro could well come to challenge the role of the US dollar in this area. The US government and the Federal Reserve have done very well over the years merely by selling dollar bills to foreigners, who have to tender real goods and services or other currencies in exchange. This seignorage (the revenue which arises because people give real goods and services to the central bank in exchange merely for cheap printed money) is fiercely protected by the US Fed. It even issued full-colour posters in Russian recently showing potential clients how they could distinguish the new $100 bills from forgeries.

Foreign holdings of dollar bills accounted for more than half of all $375 billion in issue outside banks at end 1995, and provide annual savings of $10–15 billion in interest on US Treasury securities. Without foreigners' willingness to hold stocks of greenbacks in their bedsocks, the US would have to pay interest on borrowing instead.[29] The European Central Bank is clearly interested in gaining market share in this area, as it has printed a €500 banknote. This is of limited use except to foreigners, Russian mafiosi among them, who like large denomination folding stuff to facilitate cash trades. It seems likely that the euro will displace the dollar as a useful means of exchange, particularly in eastern Europe. European taxpayers will then begin to benefit from some of these gains.

The impact of more attractive securities markets, and of a shift to holding the euro as cash should be that any putative deficit in the euro area's balance of payments will be even easier to finance. However, the euro area is currently broadly in balance on the current account of the balance-of-payments and is a substantial net creditor (in that it owns more foreign assets than it has foreign liabilities), so that this issue is

academic at present. All participants will benefit from this strong bal-ance-of-payments position, even if they themselves have traditionally been weak in this area.

Summary

This chapter has listed some of the advantages of the euro that will benefit Britain along with all other euro members. The euro is making a reality of the single market, and enabling gains in efficiency, scale and specialisation. As a result it is increasing prospective returns on invest-ment. This is one of three mechanisms by which investment, growth and jobs are increasing. The reduction of exchange-rate uncertainty is increasing cross-border investment. Reduced risk should also allow reduced interest rates in Britain taking the cycle as a whole. The cre-ation of Europe-wide capital markets is reducing the cost of funds for business expansion. This process may be boosted by a shift of investors from dollar-based to euro-based assets, and also by the advantages of issuing a currency internationally used as a means of exchange. For countries like Britain which have traditionally been bedevilled by balance-of-payments problems and sterling crises, the euro also offers the tantalising hope of unimpeded growth.

3 Britain's case

Monetary union is a system in which all can win, and Britain is no exception. But there are nevertheless some specific effects of EMU for Britain which may make the benefits particularly important, and which arise out of our particular attributes. This chapter looks at some of the features of the British economy that might be affected by membership of the euro. The most important is probably our success in attracting foreign direct investment (FDI), which is particularly impressive for one of the larger EU member states. Another feature is Britain's dependence on financial and business services, which make up 24 per cent of GDP.[30] These too may be expected to benefit particularly from Britain's euro membership. This chapter also deals with the claim that Britain might become liable for the pension fund liabilities of other euro area members, and considers the important question of how Britain would manage its currency in the new world of the euro if sterling is not to join.

Foreign direct investment

Overall, the British economy has been internationalised more rapidly than others over the last fifteen years. Our outflows of direct investment have been even more substantial than our inflows, leading to a positive net balance of foreign assets in the form of direct investment.[31] However, there is no necessary connection between the outflows and the inflows. Countries can have substantial outflows which are unmatched by inflows. Germany is currently a case where outflows outstrip inflows. So Britain's success in winning over foreign investors is impressive. Indeed, Britain had inward investment worth 28.5 per cent of GDP in 1995, more than double the EU average of 13.2 per

cent of GDP.[32] As we shall see, this success has been fundamentally as a result of Britain's EU membership, and it is now threatened by the failure to participate in the euro.

These inflows of direct investment have revolutionised manufacturing, boosting investment and productivity and introducing many working practices which had been unheard of in hidebound parts of British industry. According to Department of Trade and Industry estimates, foreign investment accounts for 26 per cent of manufacturing output, 35 per cent of manufacturing investment and 43 per cent of manufacturing exports. Toyota and Nissan have built big greenfield sites. Ford has bought Jaguar and VW has bought Rolls-Royce and Bentley. Many have embarked on or promise substantial investment programmes. But the phenomenon goes well beyond the car industry and manufacturing. Sony makes televisions in Bridgend, Wales. Intel makes microchips in Scotland. McDonald's makes hamburgers everywhere. American firms account for 3,500 plants in the United Kingdom, German firms for 1,000 and Japanese firms for 225.

Britain's success in attracting FDI appears to have continued during the 1990s. Between 1994 and 1999 Britain won 24 per cent of all the inward investment into the EU, although its GDP accounts for just 14 per cent of the EU total. This is the most impressive performance of any of the larger EU member states, including Spain.[33] There are two reasons for this. The first is that a steadily rising share of British inward investment is being undertaken by companies in other EU countries; the process of integrating supply chains from one EU country to another is continuing. The share of inward investment into the United Kingdom that comes from other European countries rose from less than 10 per cent in the early 1960s to more than 30 per cent in the 1980s and 1990s.[34]

The second is Britain's disproportionate share of FDI coming into the EU, mainly from Japanese and American companies. In 1998 we attracted 55 per cent of the total, more than three times as much as might have been expected if FDI had been spread throughout Europe

on the basis of shares in GDP. (In 1995, our share of American and Japanese FDI in the EU was 25.8 per cent, or double our GDP share. The figures bounce around because investments are often large, but the picture of disproportionate success is clear.)

Britain is seen as part of core of EU

There are many reasons for this attraction to Britain, including the use of English, the existence of a comparatively cheap labour force, and even the provision of golf courses – a distinct plus point for Japanese managers. But a crucial reason, a necessary if not sufficient condition, is that Britain is seen as part of the core of the European Union. Anything that casts doubt on that status, and this must include the decision to stay out of the launch of the European currency, is bound to foment doubts about us in the minds of some business people. Indeed, executives of various foreign investors, notably Toyota, General Motors, Daimler-Benz and Siemens, have stated the obvious (although usually hedging about their concerns as soon as press attention became unwelcome).

The most comprehensive survey of inward investors was carried out by the Centre for Economics and Business Research in 1992. It concluded that for the increasing proportion of inward investors for whom investment in Britain was as a base to supply the entire European market, Britain's participation in the euro was important in ensuring a continuing flow of investment.[35] But this is not just a matter of surveys, conjecture or anecdote; it is also the evidence of history. Before the European Union was set up by the Treaty of Rome in 1957 Britain's share of FDI into the countries of the Community was about 40 per cent. It then declined dramatically to 15 per cent over the period when we were outside from 1958 to 1973, and then it climbed up again.[36]

At present, most business people, including prospec[tive] direct investors, believe that Britain will join the single cu[rrency] that perception were to change we might well begin t[o]

building investment that has done so much to revive some of the poorest and most depressed regions of the country, including South Wales, the North-west and the North-east. More than half of the jobs created by inward direct investment have gone to these comparatively poor areas, and foreign investment has been largely responsible for their regeneration and diversification away from declining industries such as textiles, shipbuilding and coal. If we fail to join the euro we will lose one of the most important motors of prosperity of the last twenty years.

The first evidence that there is a damaging effect from Britain staying out of the euro was published in a survey from the accountancy and consulting firm Ernst and Young recently. The survey looked at new investment in plant and machinery (as opposed, say, to the foreign purchase of more than 10 per cent of the equity of a British firm, which also counts as foreign direct investment). It found that Britain's share of the EU total had fallen from 28 per cent in 1998 to 24 per cent in 1999. France's share had risen from 12 per cent in 1998 to 18 per cent in 1999. Indeed, foreign direct investment in the euro area countries as a whole rose by 11 per cent, while it fell in the 'out' countries by 18 per cent. A failure to join the single currency, within the time horizon of most business investment decisions, is likely to hit foreign direct investment.

Financial services

Apart from Britain's prowess in attracting FDI, the other peculiarity of the British economy which may be affected by EMU is financial services, particularly the wholesale markets centred on the City of London. Britain already has a high share of GDP coming from the FIREB (finance, insurance, real estate and business services) industries, which reflects the early liberalisation of this sector during the 1980s together with the diminution of state support for earnings in retirement. As a result Britain's institutional investors (insurers and pension funds) control the third largest amount of money under man-

agement of any economy in the world. The focus of this subsector of the financial industry is the equity and bond markets centred on London. Indeed, London and the South-east region are particularly dependent on the high-growth, high-income financial sector, together accounting for half of the United Kingdom's GDP generated in financial services.[37]

The City has become a magnet for foreign financial firms, and the rest of the European Union has made a significant contribution to the influx. According to a recent study by the Centre for Economic and Business Research, the number of EU-based banks with subsidiaries or branches in the City grew from 100 in 1975 to 241 in 1997, and just over half are full subsidiaries employing 22,800 staff.[38] The twenty-four German banks in London now employ 8,800 people and the eighteen French banks employ 5,800. Several big continental banks, notably Deutsche Bank and Union Bank of Switzerland, are focusing their investment banking operations on London rather than Frankfurt or Zürich.

London banks service much of EU

These institutions are involved in international business of all sorts, but banks in London are increasingly servicing an EU-wide hinterland. Overall, a recent study for the Corporation of London shows that the proportion of City turnover originating in other EU member states is now 16.5 per cent. The share is highest for international banking, where it is 37 per cent. The proportion is also high in corporate finance (that is, advice on funding for companies), equities, derivatives, foreign exchange and professional services.[39] The study estimates that about 41,000 jobs out of a City total of 250,000 are dependent on the rest of the EU. Fortunately, little of this business was associated with exchange-rate transactions between European currencies that have now disappeared.

The conventional wisdom is that the City will continue to be the dominant financial centre in the European time zone whether Britain

joins the euro or not. There are powerful effects at work. Once a business has sunk investment into an area it is reluctant to move. The fact that so much business is done in the City means that there is an incentive to do even more business there, because of easy access to investors, investment bankers, legal advisers, accountants, insurers and all the other infrastructure which grows up whenever people intensively practise a particular trade. Moreover, it is part of the City's own folklore that it became an international financial centre again at the end of the 1960s only because of heavy-handed regulation in New York. The burden of banking and financial market supervision on Wall Street made London a more attractive place to deposit and lend dollars, and the eurodollar market was born. A number of City people believe that any similar attempt to over-regulate the euro area could redound to the City's advantage.

There is, though, a certain amount of whistling to keep your spirits up in this sort of attitude. If Britain were to stay out of the euro area there would certainly be no dramatic effects on London unless the government were to score some dramatic own goal such as agreeing a withholding tax on interest. But it seems at least likely that London would be unable to capitalise on the opportunity to become Europe's financial centre, or to become what New York is to the United States. This could be a substantial missed opportunity. We have already discussed, in Chapter 2, the likely development of integrated European capital markets as investors are able to shop for the best buys across the whole euro area without taking exchange-rate risks. Given the advantages of critical mass in financial markets, it is likely that these markets will gradually converge on one centre. This should be London.

EU funds management is a growing area

If we look at the areas where EU business is least significant for London the management of EU funds comes lowest.[40] This is partly because there are fewer institutional funds to manage in France and Germany, which together account for about $2.2 trillion compared

with $1.7 trillion under management in Britain.[41] But this will change over the next ten years as both countries move away from state provision for retirement and the trend that has already been observed in Britain and the United States sets in. Given the size of the French and German economies, and the high savings rates, their institutional funds are likely to overtake those available in Britain fairly rapidly as soon as pension reform gets under way. If Britain is outside the euro area it seems inherently less plausible that it will be able to enjoy the lion's share of domestically generated business.

After all, the focus of the euro money markets is in Frankfurt, which is where the decisions on interest rates are taken. This is therefore also becoming the focus for the bond market, as judgements on short-term policy interest rates crucially affect the perception of longer-term, fixed-interest securities. The idea that Frankfurt will be as insignificant as Washington, the headquarters of the US Federal Reserve, overlooks the fact that Frankfurt already has substantial financial markets whereas Washington has none. No other monetary area has ever seen its principal financial markets grow up in a country outside the jurisdiction of its banking supervisors, and it is hard to imagine that the euro area policymakers would be happy to see this happen if Britain did not participate.

The euro participants have already been reluctant to allow London-based banks to participate fully in TARGET, a settlement system for euro financial institutions. Moreover, the continent's financial exchanges have shown their ability to win substantial volumes back from London. The Deutsche Terminboerse (DTB), Frankfurt's stock exchange, slashed the costs of trading futures contracts in German bunds (government bonds) and won the volume back from the London International Financial Futures Exchange (LIFFE). The London Stock Exchange seems to have recognised the threat to its position by attempting to agree joint ventures, at one stage (now failed) agreeing to set up a joint venture with the DTB in which, despite London's vastly greater market value, the German exchange would have had a 50 per cent stake.

Nor should the City or British policymakers rely on a level playing field. The financial authorities in France, in particular, take an interventionist view about promoting Paris as a financial centre. When the City began to trade the majority of deals in French government bonds in the late 1980s the then head of the French Trésor, Jean-Claude Trichet, launched a fierce campaign to repatriate the bond market to Paris. The securities were streamlined to make them easier to buy and sell. The Trésor also conducted a major marketing campaign, and it is reputed to have put the word around the French banks that it would take a dim view if they continued to trade in bulk through London. Within months the market had shifted back to Paris.

The opportunity for the City to become the centre of the euro area's financial markets – rather as New York is the centre of the US markets – also depends on EU legislation. If a single market in financial services is to be created, some forty separate measures (forming the Commission's financial services action plan) including twenty laws have to be passed. These will remove many of the national obstacles to financial services from other member states: for example, the requirement to meet national conditions on what should be in the prospectus of an initial public offering, or the requirement that a certain minimum of government bonds be held in a private pensions portfolio. In principle, the City's wholesale market would be the greatest beneficiary of these changes. Moreover, there is a commitment to passing these laws by 2005, the deadline set at the Lisbon summit.

However, there must be a serious risk that the necessary legislation will be particularly shaped to meet the perceived interests of the euro area members rather than the EU as a whole. After all, the degree of cross-border business is likely to be far greater within the euro-area than in 'outs' like Britain. This is in part because all the legislation can be passed by a qualified majority in the Council of Ministers (71 per cent of the votes) plus the assent of the European Parliament.[42] The necessary majorities exist within the euro group (the euro 12) as they are at present. Moreover, the degree of cross-border business is likely to

be far greater within the euro area than with any EU members outside, not least because it is an objective of the system to ensure that bank transfers can be made as cheaply within the whole area as within any member state. It is, of course, possible that the euro group will be the first monetary area in history to pass legislation designed to locate their principal financial markets outside their jurisdiction. But that is not the sort of altruism traditionally displayed by states.

In addition, there is likely over time to be an increasing case for a financial services authority across the euro area as banks and financial markets become more integrated, and as cross-border services are also speeded by the advent of e-commerce. Were the EU member states to vote to establish a common supervisory framework, reflecting their greater integration, it seems highly unlikely that it would come to London, despite the importance of the City to European financial services, if the UK were not a euro area member. The Lamfalussy group of wise men, appointed in 2000 to look at this area, argued first for greater co-ordination of supervisors. But the real integration of EU markets was only just beginning.

In conclusion, the City has great strengths which will not be eroded quickly. Both Frankfurt and Paris are small financial centres by comparison; as British officials point out, there are more people merely employed in financial services in London than live in Frankfurt. But a decision to stay out of the euro area for any length of time would undoubtedly chip away at London's dominance, and would increasingly lead to missed opportunities as the euro area markets developed elsewhere. Much of the talk on this subject misses the point. The threat to London's role as an offshore international centre is perhaps less significant than the opportunity to develop London as the true financial centre for its continent, in the same way as New York is the key financial centre for the United States.

Do the real opportunities lie elsewhere?
Against these points some Eurosceptics argue that there is no point in

integrating Britain even further into Europe because the real opportunities lie elsewhere in the high-growth markets around the world. Until the onset of the Asian regional crisis, with the devaluation of the Thai baht in July 1997, a favourite candidate for the Eurosceptics was the high-growth economies of Asia-Pacific.[43] These economies do have real strengths that will ensure that they recover before long and resume their growth. But the idea that we should ignore Europe, even though it has traditionally been more slow-growing than the Asian economies, is absurd.

The rest of the European Union took 53 per cent of our total exports of goods and services in 1999, whereas all developing economies put together, not just Asia-Pacific but Latin America, the oil-producing economies and developing Europe as well, took 21 per cent.[44] Simple arithmetic shows that the growth rate of exports to the developing world would have to be nearly three times the growth rate of exports to the European Union to provide the same absolute increase in sales and jobs. Moreover, the argument that Britain should either integrate with Europe or pursue opportunities in Asia is fundamentally flawed. In truth, we can and should do both. The more successful we are in the European single market, the more attractive our products are likely to be in world markets outside. If we do well in Europe we will do better in Asia. Economics is not a game where you only win if someone loses.

Unfunded pension liabilities

Another common Eurosceptic misconception is that somehow Britain, if it were to join the single European currency, would ultimately become liable for vast hidden liabilities incurred by other European countries. The most compelling candidate in this saga is the so-called unfunded pension liabilities, the extent to which countries are not raising enough in taxation or social-security obligations to meet the promises that they have made to future pensioners. Various estimates of these unfunded liabilities have been made. One of the more author-

itative was done in the mid-nineties by the IMF and suggested that Britain's unfunded liabilities amounted to just 19 per cent of GDP, compared with 98 per cent of GDP in France, 113 per cent in Italy and 139 per cent in Germany.[45]

These calculations are now very out of date, but it is important nevertheless to be clear what they represent since they have had such wide circulation in the UK. They project the future pensioner population, and then they project what those pensioners will be paid, over and above what will be coming into the exchequer in contributions, if present pension policies remain in place. Lastly, they work out the sum of money that would be necessary for a government to invest now if it were to pay all those extra unfunded pensions out of its investment.[46]

The point about these so-called unfunded liabilities is that they are not a debt but an analytical tool for telling us that pensions policy is unsustainable. Another way of expressing the same concept is to look at the tax and contribution rate which would be necessary to fund the rise in pensions dictated by present policies and the demographic trends of an ageing population. It is almost the definition of the state's role in the economy that it should take on commitments that involve too much uncertainty for the private sector. But we do not look at the unfunded liability involved in educating all future generations of school children, or of defending the realm, or of providing health care. But if we were to perform the same calculation for the National Health Service – working out the sum of money needed to ensure that its present spending growth could continue for ever – we would find a huge unfunded liability. But we do not do any such calculation. So it is important not to become overawed by these apparently large numbers or to confuse them with real and much more contractually enforceable debts.

Used as an analytical tool, calculations of unfunded liabilities or projected contribution rates can be a spur to reform. We now have many examples of governments which have reformed their pension systems precisely to diminish or abolish this problem. Indeed, Britain

used to have an enormous unfunded pension liability because the state pension used to rise in line with earnings and there was a state earnings-related pension supplement (SERPS). Margaret Thatcher cut this unfunded liability in one fell swoop by linking the basic future old-age pension to prices rather than earnings and by curbing SERPS.

On the continent, substantial progress has been made to curb unsustainable pension commitments, although for understandable political reasons, politicians do not usually shout about such cuts from the rooftops. Italy for example has introduced two important state pension reforms that have lengthened the number of contribution years needed to draw a pension, and cut the pension offered. The OECD has calculated that a continuation of the pre-1992 policy in Italy would have led to a peak of pensions spending at 23 per cent of GDP. After the Amato reforms in 1992, this was cut to 18.5 per cent of GDP. And after the Dini reforms of 1995, the peak was calculated at 15.5 per cent of GDP.[47] In May 1999, the Italian government ended double taxation of pension income in order to encourage private pension provision.

The German government embarked on an important pension reform, the Riester reform, during 2000. Although the cuts in state pensions and the new tax incentives for private pensions are controversial, particularly with the German trade unions, most analysts expect them to pass. Only in France is there no serious attempt to reform the pensions system, but that arises partly from the fact that France has a smaller ageing problem. Indeed, some experts argue that its public pension system may well prove to be sustainable with just the modest changes on which the Jospin government has embarked.[48] The most thorough recent study of the problem, undertaken jointly by the EU governments' Treasury officials, shows that pension spending as a percentage of GDP is projected to remain stable in Britain and to rise to its peak by only 1.7 percentage points of GDP in Italy, 3.9 percentage points of GDP in France, and by 4.3 per cent in Germany.[49]

The attempt to suggest, as the Eurosceptics have repeatedly done,

that Britain might become liable for other countries' pensions is as mischievous and misleading as suggesting that they might become liable for our unfunded National Health Service liabilities. (After all, the NHS is badly affected by an ageing population and has no funds of its own.) They ignore the article in the Maastricht Treaty which clearly forbids one public authority from bailing out another. Article 103 states: 'A member state shall not be liable for or assume the commitments of central governments, regional, local or other public authorities, other bodies governed by public law, or public undertakings of another member state.'

The world will change

There is a final point about the specific nature of Britain's case which the Eurosceptics overlook. They assume that Britain can opt for a world which remains broadly unchanged from the one that we are in today, despite the creation of the euro. In fact, the existence of such a large currency, encompassing thirteen economies with a combined GDP only a little short of that of the United States, is likely to complicate British monetary policy if we remain outside.

Nearly half of Britain's trade is with the thirteen members of the euro area. Imports from the euro area account for 50 per cent of all imports of goods and services, and therefore nearly half of the inflationary impact of any rise or fall in the pound will originate with the euro area and the euro. This is nearly four times as much as the importance to inflation of American imports. But it is also true that short-term capital flows move the pound up and down in line with the dollar. So we may find the pound moving sharply with the dollar and making life extremely bumpy for all those who depend on continental markets. Moreover, the volatility of the exchange rate between the euro and the dollar is likely to be much greater than it is at present, because the European Central Bank is likely to care much less about movements in the external value of the currency as imports will be a comparatively small share of the euro area. The euro area's exports of goods and

services account for 16 per cent of GDP, only a little more than exports in the United States or Japan. The euro area is a continent-wide marketplace of a similar size to the United States, and its policymakers are thus less worried about movements in its exchange rate than ours.[50]

It could therefore be hard for the neighbours of the euro to hang on to its coat-tails, even though it will be more important for their own inflation and trade competitiveness that they do. Like it or not, the British economy will be more intimately dependent on the euro area and its currency than any other area. As a result British policymakers' tolerance of sharp movements against the euro is likely to be low. Yet closely fixing the exchange rate against the euro – an updated exchange rate mechanism – is not a realistic option given today's volatile capital flows. Combined with the probability that the euro will be volatile against the dollar, British interest rates may have to move up and down to reduce the movement of the pound against the euro. Join it or not, the euro will be too big to ignore.

Summary

This chapter has looked at the special importance of the euro for the maintenance of Britain's good record on FDI and the position of financial services within the economy. In both cases there are sound reasons for believing that a decision to adopt the euro will benefit Britain, whereas a decision to stay out will increasingly endanger these traditional advantages. It also examined the argument that Britain would have to assume the unfunded pension liabilities of other euro participants, and pointed out the progress in reducing these so-called liabilities and how different they are from debt. In addition, the Maastricht Treaty prohibits any bail-out of one government by others. Lastly, it considered the increased difficulties British policymakers are likely to face if we do not join as a result of our intimate dependence on the euro area and the euro.

4 The disadvantages of the euro

Since this is the section of the book advocating the euro, you might expect to see a short chapter on its disadvantages. That it is comparatively long is a tribute to the ability of the British to look gift horses in the mouth and to be much better at pointing out small flaws than spotting big advantages. The critics are particularly blind to the benefits of reduced risk, greater scale economies and more efficiency of EMU. It is noticeable that business people and business economists are much more aware of these advantages than the academic critics. Of course, there are disadvantages of the euro to place in the scales. But they are small and are likely to diminish over time. The balance of benefits and costs therefore weighs heavily in favour of our membership.

The critics argue that EMU either cannot work or will work badly because the European economies are too different to accept the same interest rate and the same exchange rate, which is an inevitable consequence of EMU. In their view, a one-size-fits-all monetary policy will lead to breakdown and disaster. In the jargon, they contend that Europe is not an 'optimum currency area'. However, this is largely based on a misunderstanding, because no existing country is an optimum currency area. Currencies have been adopted not because they suit particular regions that trade a lot with each other, but because of political boundaries that may originally have been drawn up on the whim of a medieval marriage settlement. Embarrassingly for the Eurosceptics, the Nobel prize-winning father of this whole field of economics and of the idea of optimum currency areas, Professor Robert Mundell, recently backed Europe's adoption of the euro and accused his critics of misunderstanding him. He argued that the euro's benefits would clearly outweigh the costs.[51]

...f an independent monetary policy. Can one size fit all?

...his chapter will show that the differences between euro regions are within the bounds that exist in other monetary unions, such as the United States, Germany and Britain itself. One interest rate and exchange rate can fit all. If a monetary union for Europe is inappropriate, then a monetary union is also inappropriate for parts of Britain, notably Northern Ireland and East Anglia, and there should be separate currencies for different parts of Britain too. But this would be a nonsense. The benefits of a separate monetary policy – of a separate national interest rate and exchange rate – are more limited than often supposed, and they have on several occasions proved to be a disadvantage.

It is often said that Britain's business cycle is more similar to that in the United States than to the continental cycle, and that this is a serious obstacle to sharing an interest rate with the continent. Indeed, a recent International Monetary Fund working paper agreed that the UK cycle has been more correlated with North America than Europe over the period from 1960 to 1997.[52] But a correlation without an explanation does not mean much, and the explanation implies nothing for our euro membership. Nearly half of the forty year period was dominated by the long 1980s boom and its early 1990s aftermath, and it was a pure coincidence that both Britain and the United States had reforming market-oriented governments at the same time. Both President Reagan and Prime Minister Thatcher liberalised financial markets, made borrowing easier, and encouraged a sharp rise in consumer spending and growth. But that synchronised cycle does not mean that it will happen again.

The IMF authors found that the British business cycle had been 'more volatile than, and relatively independent of, the cycle in the euro area countries'. But was this a good thing? We suffered nine recessions – defined as two consecutive quarters of falling output – compared with six in Italy or the United States, four in Germany and two in France. Of the three common recessions, in 1973–5, 1980–82 and

1990–93, Britain managed to have both the deepest and the longest downturns of any of the leading six western nations in two of the three episodes, and the second deepest and longest (after Italy) in 1973–5. The explanation was telling. The authors identified 'a relatively significant role for monetary policy in explaining these differences'. In other words, our own interest-rate policy has been a source of our volatility. We have been scoring own goals. Far from being a useful lever, separate interest rates and exchange rates have been a source of sorry temptation to the British political class.

What, though, happens if a shock hits Britain but not the rest of the monetary union (in other words, the shock is asymmetric)? Let us assume that a health scare hits British food production at the same time as a terrorist outrage hits tourism. People are thrown out of work. We need to boost other parts of the economy to increase the jobs to replace those lost in food and tourism, and we need to increase our exports to pay for the same level of imports. Nowadays, the Bank of England might simply cut interest rates and allow the pound to fall. Both movements would help the economy to adjust to the change in circumstances.

In principle, the loss of an independent monetary policy is a disadvantage in these circumstances. But how likely are these different shocks? A substantial amount of work has been done on whether the European economies behave in a similar manner to each other. The pioneering research in this field suggested that output in Austria, Belgium, Denmark, France, Greece, the Netherlands and Spain was relatively closely aligned with Germany over the period 1964–90.[53] However, Finland, Ireland, Italy, Portugal, Sweden and the United Kingdom were less closely linked with Germany. The interesting point, though, is that all the European countries had closer links with Germany than parts of the United States had with each other. The link in the United States between the core Mid-east and the South West and the Rocky Mountains is particularly low, but the US monetary ion survives and prospers.[54]

In one important respect, this study did an injustice to both the European and the US monetary unions because it implicitly assumed that the monetary authorities set interest rates for a core area and ignored the rest. A crucial advantage of EMU over the traditional European fixed exchange-rate system revolving around the German Bundesbank's decisions is that the European Central Bank (ECB) takes account of developments throughout the region, not just in Germany. Therefore the real test of appropriateness should be whether GDP growth moves in line with the average, not with some other part. This has been calculated for three different periods by the Organisation for Economic Co-operation and Development (OECD) and is shown in Table 4.1.

These figures show that the European economies move closely in line with each other, apart from in the middle period (1987–92H1) when Germany was out of line with the average. The reason for the divergence was Germany's unification in 1989. At that time the German economy was being boosted by an expansionary fiscal policy as the government decided that some of the costs of unification should be met by borrowing and therefore shared with future generations. This put pressure on the Bundesbank to raise interest rates to offset the impact on demand, which caused other European countries to raise their interest rates to keep in line with the Deutschmark.

If the euro had been operating there would have been no such rise in interest rates (although Germany would have suffered overheating and extra inflation instead). The real point, though, is that German unification is the sort of economic shock which, by definition, will never happen again. It was a one-off, and it would be foolish to construct monetary arrangements on the assumption that such shocks will frequently occur given the other advantages of a single currency. If we look at the other periods the correlations appear surprisingly high, although they do break the euro area into a group of countries that move together strongly (Austria, Belgium, France, Germany, the Netherlands and, surprisingly, Italy) and the others.

Table 4.1 **GDP growth correlations with the prospective euro area**

	1977–86	1987–92H1	1992H2–96
Germany	0.89	0.28	0.93
France	0.72	0.85	0.99
Italy	0.93	0.65	0.92
Austria	0.65	0.71	0.85
Belgium	0.51	0.92	0.97
Finland	0.17	0.68	0.88
Ireland	0.30	0.65	0.76
Netherlands	0.76	0.60	0.89
Portugal	0.48	0.43	0.41
Spain	0.21	0.62	0.94
United Kingdom	0.48	0.53	0.57
Denmark	0.33	-0.07	0.54
Greece	0.65	0.36	0.83
Sweden	0.27	0.61	0.90

Note. Correlations are based on semi-annual data and are with the EMU 11 area.
H stands for half.
Source: OECD secretariat.

The most fashionable argument for the assertion that one interest rate does not fit all concerns the experience of Ireland. The prominent Eurosceptic economist Professor Patrick Minford, for example, has argued that Ireland faces inflation of 10 per cent for three years thanks to its inability to set a national interest rate.[55] The perspective from Dublin – or indeed any other vantage point unaffected by the cavalier treatment of facts in the British debate – looks rather different. True, Ireland's EU measure of inflation in the autumn of 2000 had risen to 6 per cent compared with an average 2.7 per cent in the euro area as a whole. However, a slice of that increase was due to one-off factors that

have nothing to do with the demand pressures within the Irish economy. The finance minister raised cigarette duties in the December 1999 budget adding nearly 1 percentage point to the consumer inflation rate, and the fall of the euro (and hence the Irish punt) pushed up import prices particularly sharply in Ireland. This is because of the close links between the Irish and British economies. Ireland's imports are worth half of GDP, and more than 80 per cent of them come from outside the euro area (mainly Britain and the United States). Both these effects began to drop out of the year-on-year comparison of prices, and hence the inflation rate fell back more rapidly than many expected in the early part of 2001.[56] The OECD forecast in November 2000 for Irish inflation projected that it would fall back to below 5 per cent in 2001 and would average 3.8 per cent in 2002.

There is also a fundamental economic point about diverging inflation rates in a monetary union. They are part of the mechanism by which real adjustments continue to be made. Relatively poor countries that are catching up with their richer partners are likely over time to have a modestly higher inflation rate. This is known as the Balassa-Samuelson effect:[57] productivity gains tend to be concentrated in the trading sectors, which therefore stay competitive even though they pay good wage increases. But these wage increases have to be matched by other employers in the economy with fewer productivity gains, so they have to pass them on in higher prices. Therefore the inflation rate in high productivity growth economies, where the productivity gains are concentrated in, say, manufacturing, tends to be higher than the average. This does not imply any loss of competitiveness. Hong Kong, for example, has had a fixed exchange rate with the dollar for many years with much higher inflation rates than the United States. But it did not lose competitiveness thanks to the productivity gains in the trading sectors.

There may also be substantial difference in inflation within a monetary union reflecting differing economic conditions, but this is no more than a temporary phenomenon. The Bureau of Labor Statistics in the

United States has maintained price data from seventeen US cities over the whole period from 1919 to 1998. During that time, the difference between the minimum and the maximum inflation rates reached more than 8 percentage points in the early 1920s, 6 percentage points in the early 1930s and 7 percentage points in the early 1980s. Overall, a difference of about 2 percentage points is typical. A recent study by the European Central Bank concluded that 'the magnitude of these differentials observed in recent years … is very close to the magnitudes prevailing in the euro area'.[58] Differences in inflation rates are a sign of the market making necessary adjustments and are a normal part of any monetary union. It is, however, inconceivable that inflation could simply take off in one part of a monetary union, leaving the price level elsewhere behind. Competition and trade ensure that prices for tradeable commodities cannot get too far out of line.

European economies are becoming more integrated

There is one other message from the research on the links between the European economies: it is clear that the European economies are moving together more often today than used to be the case. This is not surprising. As we shall see, the European economies are becoming steadily more integrated with each other. It is noticeable that Britain no longer looks as lonely as it does if compared merely with the German economy. Britain and the euro area as a whole move together quite happily, and the links are increasing. Thus a single interest rate and exchange rate are likely to become ever more comfortable for the United Kingdom. Moreover, this work underestimates the ease with which Britain would fit into the euro because the correlation is calculated with the average of the eleven rather than the twelve, as it would be with Britain as a member. If Britain joined, European monetary policy would take account of monetary conditions in Britain as well as elsewhere.

There is another way of thinking about how appropriate the euro would be, which is to look at the diversity within the euro area

compared with the diversity between regions within existing member states (or effective monetary unions). Here the surprising result of some interesting new research is that, for Germany and Britain, the correlation with the euro area as a whole is likely to be as appropriate as the monetary unions which exist now between national regions and their national economies.[59] For example, Britain's economy is more closely linked with the euro area than either East Anglia's or Northern Ireland's economies are with Britain. If Britain is thought to be too divergent to participate in the euro then the same logic would suggest that there should be separate currencies for East Anglia and Northern Ireland. The study also shows that British regions are no more divergent from the euro area average than German regions, with the sole exception of Northern Ireland.

My overall conclusion from these studies is that Britain may have to adjust a little more than the core countries, and may therefore lose a little more than some other potential participants from the loss of a separate interest rate and exchange rate. Britain is not part of the core group for which a common interest rate and exchange rate are likely to prove most comfortable, and there may be periods in which European monetary policy is inappropriate for British needs. But the loss is well within the bounds already shown to be practicable by the experience of both the United States and Britain's own regions. It would also be handsomely offset by the other benefits likely to arise as a result of our membership of the euro.

Different cultures are not a barrier to monetary union

James Forder airily dismisses all this research as irrelevant on the grounds that, however well integrated Europe's economies are, Europeans simply do not have the fellow feeling which will allow periods in which European interest rates or the euro exchange rate will be inappropriate. This vastly overestimates the extent to which interest rates are likely to become a political issue, a misjudgement which is understandable given Britain's sad inflationary and interest-rate history.

When inflation is high and rising, interest rates have to be higher and to rise faster. But this view is far too pessimistic for countries with reasonably low inflation and stable interest rates. The euro area is, in this respect, much more like Germany than Britain. Interest rates will not vary much, and they will therefore not become a political issue in the way they have in Britain.

We also have many examples throughout the world of countries composed of substantially different cultural and ethnic groups which are nevertheless in a monetary union. Within Europe, Switzerland is a stable monetary union despite its four language groups and independent cantons. Belgium has three languages and shares a currency with Luxembourg. Outside Europe there are more examples. China has many different languages, albeit sharing common written ideograms. India has more than ten major languages and two language groups as different as romance and teutonic languages in Europe. South Africa contains speakers of Xhosa, Zulu, Afrikaans and English. All of these multi-ethnic societies survive more or less happily with a single currency.

Trade patterns

Moreover, all the work on the linkages between the European economies, on which we can base a judgement about the applicability of a common monetary policy, is based on past history which underestimates the growing linkages between the European economies. In Britain's case, for example, the trade share of GDP with other EU members rose from 3.3 per cent of GDP in 1960 to more than 12 per cent in the mid-1990s. This increasing integration is being reinforced by a change in the nature of trade. Traditional trade has been in products where countries have particular advantages; for example, Scotland exports whisky and buys bananas from the Windward Islands. In both cases the production process is almost exclusively in those countries, which makes them independent of each other and liable to differing external shocks. A blight on the banana crop would not affect Scotland at all.

But modern trade is increasingly about trade among businesses in the same industry. German and Swedish car makers buy components from British-based Lucas and GKN, Sony buys components from Thomson of France to make televisions in Wales, and so on. These trends have made the structure of all developed economies, particularly the European economies because they are more integrated, more similar over the years. Developed economies are becoming less prone to shocks which will define the fortunes of one compared with another. A shock which affects the European car industry – say, a sudden shift in consumer tastes towards Detroit-produced gas guzzlers – is likely to affect the euro area fairly evenly. In these circumstances one monetary policy – one interest rate and exchange rate – can help make the adjustment that is necessary.[60] So there are sound reasons for believing that the extent to which the European economies will move together will grow, even without the additional incentives of the integration brought about by the euro itself.

Nor is the existing structure of external trade much different among the larger member states. The most common way of looking at the structure of trade is to examine the proportion of exports that go to particular destinations, and this shows that Britain's share of exports outside the euro area is some 50 per cent compared with Germany's 55 per cent or Italy's 52 per cent.[61] However, the more significant measure of a country's exposure to developments in a particular region of the world is to look at its exports to that area as a proportion of total output. After all, it does not much matter if a country exports a high proportion of its exports to a particular country if its exports are actually an insignificant part of total output. Table 4.2 shows trade outside and inside the euro area 13 (including Greece, and assuming Britain is also a member) as a share of GDP. The main message is surely that the trade share is surprisingly similar for the big member states. Britain is less exposed to non-euro area trade than Belgium, Finland, Ireland, Germany, Austria or the Netherlands, all of which are first-wave members. The conventional wisdom, that Britain trades more outside

Table 4.2 **Export exposure to the euro area and outside***

	Ranking of non-euro area exports (% of GDP 1999)	*Exports to euro area (% of GDP)*
Ireland	28.5	46.4
Belgium	19.9	49.5
Finland	18.2	14.4
Sweden	17.6	18.0
Netherlands	13.7	40.4
Germany	12.0	13.5
Denmark	11.9	14.3
Austria	11.2	19.2
Euro 13	10.3	15.1
UK	9.2	9.1
Italy	8.7	10.9
France	8.5	13.1
Spain	5.4	12.1
Portugal	4.4	16.4
Greece	4.1	3.7

* Euro countries plus Britain, as if Britain were a Euroland member

Source: IMF Direction of Trade Statistics, International Financial Statistics.

Europe than our partners, is quite wrong. In 1999, Britain's non-euro area trade was actually below average for the euro area.[62]

Within the total of exports outside the euro area the only significant difference is that Britain exports more to the United States and less to other non-euro area markets. Britain's exports to the United States account for 2.8 per cent of GDP, whereas the euro area 13 average is 2.3 per cent of GDP. But this is hardly a significant difference within the overall picture of similarity. Of participants in EMU, Ireland and Belgium have a higher proportion of GDP going to the United States

in exports, while Finland and Germany have shares similar to that of the United Kingdom.

Some Eurosceptics argue that the UK also has a particularly high share of dollar-denominated trade compared with other EU countries. However, this should not be significant. For example, oil prices are denominated in dollars, but the price of oil depends on the supply and demand for oil, not on the supply and demand for dollars. The dollar is merely a numéraire – an accounting device. Equally, other Eurosceptics say that North Sea oil and gas is an impediment to our euro membership. However, the importance of oil and gas extraction can be overstated, as it now represents 1.7 per cent of GDP. Moreover, many producers are American companies, and their profits accrue to the United States. Within Europe, the Netherlands have similar offshore gas, and have had no trouble being a euro member. Indeed, euro membership brings the advantage of protecting the vast bulk of the trading sectors from any exchange-rate changes flowing from changes in oil and gas prices. In general, though, European economies react in the same way to oil and gas price changes. Higher prices hit consumer confidence in Britain and on the continent, as we saw during the petrol price protests in 2000.

The nature of debt

Another much-cited difficulty for the euro in general, and for Britain in particular, is the different nature of the debts in different countries. Critics say that British households are more indebted than those on the continent, and that they generally borrow at short-term interest rates. Therefore they will bear the brunt of any adjustment in European monetary policy if Britain joins. If the ECB needs to tighten policy British households will feel the pinch soonest, because their mortgage rates are linked to short-term interest rates. The most recent comparison by the Bank for International Settlements, which is rather out of date, does indeed show that the interest rates on British debt are linked to short-term interest rates. About 90 per cent of British borrowing in

1993 was at variable interest rates, compared with only 36 per cent of German borrowing and 13 per cent of French borrowing.[63]

However, this is not the end of the story. The Eurosceptics commit a classic economic error in taking into account only a part of the effects. The impact on the economy as a whole depends on the balance of savers and borrowers: for example, a rise in interest rate hits borrowers but benefits savers. There have been several attempts to assess the overall situation. They do not support the simplistic view that variable interest-rate debt could be bad news for Britain in EMU. In a recent analysis the IMF suggested that a 1 percentage point interest-rate rise leads to a fall in output of 0.7–0.9 per cent from the baseline projection of output in Austria, Belgium, Finland, Germany, the Netherlands and the United Kingdom.[64] The low point is 11–12 quarters after the tightening. In the other group of countries (Denmark, France, Italy, Portugal, Spain and Sweden), a 1 percentage point tightening leads to a smaller but more rapid decline in output; the drop is 0.4–0.6 per cent after 5–6 quarters. The most recent study at the time of writing, which encapsulates some important methodological advances, is by Professor Rudi Dornbusch and various colleagues. It suggests that there is actually rather less effect of changes in interest rates in Britain than in some other countries.[65] Their estimates suggest that the British economy will respond only two-thirds as much as France or Germany and only half as much as Italy. This is entirely contrary to the simplistic view that variable-rate mortgages will be a problem for the United Kingdom in EMU.

The evidence, therefore, is that the behaviour of the British economy when interest rates change is not much different from that of other member states. Nor is EMU likely to prove problematic, even for British individuals with high variable interest-rate debt, because interest rates are likely to prove less volatile, as we saw in Chapter 2. It is also worth remembering that the particular dependence of Britain on short-term interest rates came about in response to high inflation. (This meant that lenders would not be prepared to lend unless there

was some assurance that interest rates would move in line with inflation.) The move to EMU is likely to provide strong incentives for people to undertake borrowing at fixed interest rates for longer periods, because long-term interest rates will be lower. The ECB offers a credible commitment to low inflation in future.

Fiscal transfers

Critics of EMU also point out that there is no automatic mechanism to transfer money from parts of euro area that have not been affected by a shock to the part that has. In their view this means that the social and political strains on EMU could become intense. In other monetary unions, notably the United States, the federal tax system has the effect of cushioning problems in part of the monetary union. When Texas suffered from the fall in the oil price in 1986 it paid less income tax to Washington and it also received transfers from Washington, which pays unemployment benefit. These offsetting fiscal transfers have been estimated, in the first instance, as worth about 30 cents in every dollar of income lost in the region.[66]

However, this point ignores the fact that someone has to pay for these transfers, and that someone includes Texans. Unless a region is consistently unlucky compared with other regions, it will end up paying more tax in the good years to fund its greater receipts in the bad years. Some two-thirds of the 30 cents in the dollar which are immediately handed back to the depressed region in lower income tax receipts and higher unemployment benefit are actually just a transfer to the region today, at the cost of higher taxes over time paid by the region itself. They are an inter-temporal transfer (a transfer from future generations to the present generation by means of borrowing) not an inter-regional transfer. Only 10 cents in the dollar is genuine insurance to more volatile regions.[67]

This is highly significant because euro area countries can borrow to cushion the impact of a short-term downturn. So two-thirds of the effects of the US federal system are already available through normal

counter-cyclical borrowing by governments. Moreover, a crucial part of the insurance function will continue to be performed within national member states by their own fiscal transfer systems from one region to another. This now accounts for about half of the insurance potential of a Europe-wide system, further reducing the need for a fiscal federation.[68]

There could, of course, be a problem. What if the EU rules stop countries from borrowing? The ability of fiscal policy to offset shocks that hit only one country depends crucially on the room for manoeuvre participating member countries have within the constraints of the Maastricht Treaty and the Stability and Growth Pact.[69] This essentially commits participants to a 'medium-term objective of budgetary positions close to balance or in surplus', which will allow member states to deal with normal cyclical fluctuations 'while keeping the government deficit within the 3 per cent of GDP reference value'. If countries exceed a deficit of 3 per cent of GDP, save in exceptional circumstances such as a fall in GDP of more than 2 per cent, the Council of Ministers can levy refundable deposits (transferable into fines after two years for persistent offenders).[70]

The good news, though, is that the EMU participants' budgets are now better than for many years. All the euro area members in 2000 had enough room for manoeuvre in their budgets to stay within the 3 per cent deficit limit even if their tax revenues and welfare spending were hit by a normal recession. The strength of the underlying budget position of the participating members has been underestimated by many analysts, who became obsessed with the so-called fiddles and fudges used to flatter the figures in 1997 in order to meet the Maastricht criteria. However, member states continued to retrench even when the euro was launched, and their budgets began to reflect the higher growth in the euro area. Indeed, several euro area countries were contemplating modest tax cuts for the first time in many years.[71] In the case of Britain the budget position was already strong enough to withstand a normal recession and stay within the limits. So in principle

we should have no difficulty in meeting the criteria. Nor should we have problems staying within these criteria in a normal recession.

In fact, fiscal policy is probably more useful today in the euro area than it has been for many years, precisely because budgets are in a healthy state. For the first time since the 1960s, all the member states are able to allow their budget deficits to expand fully, if there is a recession, without fear of a financial crisis of confidence. The long-standing attempt to improve public finances in order to prepare for monetary union has yielded an important reward. Far from hobbling fiscal policy, the move towards monetary union and Maastricht has reinstated Keynesian budgetary policy as a useful stabilising influence in the new Europe.

Exchange-rate flexibility and devaluation

Although fiscal policy will continue to have a primary role in cushioning the impact of changes in the economic environment for regions (or for countries), it is not in itself a means of adjustment. It is a way of delaying and making more palatable the changes that may be necessary to adapt to changes in consumer demand or supply changes (such as competing goods which substitute for long-established ones). The adjustment ultimately has to be made by businesses and by their workforces. If an economy as a whole suffers from an adverse shock, whereby its capital and labour are underemployed, it can at present use its exchange rate to help to price those unemployed resources back into work. A fall in the exchange rate makes exports cheaper when converted into foreign currency and imports more expensive in the home currency. The loss of the exchange rate is therefore a potentially important loss for countries that participate in EMU.

However, the usefulness of exchange-rate flexibility is heavily circumscribed. Devaluations work only if they lead to a fall in the cost of production in the devaluing country even after allowing for subsequent price rises. They can work when there is substantial unemployment dampening down wage demands; this was the story of the sharp

devaluation of the pound after its exit from the ERM in 1992. However, most devaluations in Britain have not worked except in the short run. The subsequent rise in import prices has pushed up domestic consumer prices, and the trade unions and powerful groups of employees with scarce skills have rapidly won wage increases to offset these price rises. Within a fairly short period domestic prices have risen by enough to compensate for the original fall in the exchange rate. What you gain on the devaluation roundabout you rapidly lose on the inflationary swings. Devaluation buys only a short-term gain.

This ratchet – devaluation, rising import prices, rising inflation, rising wage increases, more devaluation – is why the pound has fallen so far over such a long period of time since the 1960s, while having a negligible beneficial effect on the competitiveness of British goods in home or foreign markets. As Professor David Currie has pointed out:

> In 1966 sterling traded at about DEM11. An independent monetary policy had allowed this to slip to around DEM2.3 in 1996, an average depreciation of nearly 5 per cent a year over 30 years. Monetary freedom has offered little real benefit to the United Kingdom; the principal result has been that it has experienced on average nearly 5 per cent more inflation than Germany. Moreover, the UK economy has exhibited greater instability over this period than any of its major competitors.[72]

This finding on instability is particularly interesting because it is quite likely that the operation of an independent monetary policy has actually aggravated Britain's problems, as I showed earlier in this chapter when discussing independent monetary policy. Certainly, the pursuit of strict monetary targets in the period 1979–81 helped to impart a serious economic shock to the economy. The Barber boom and then the reaction to the 1973–4 oil-price shock were also subject to widespread criticism, leaving Britain with a far higher inflation rate than its competitors. So it would be wrong to see monetary policy and

devaluation solely as a way of helping to respond to adverse shocks. The operation of monetary policy in Britain has actually been a significant source of such shocks. The cure has sometimes proved worse than the disease.

Over time the usefulness of the devaluation option, even if it is operated positively and helpfully, is also being eroded. As an economy becomes more open to trade the impact of a fall in the exchange rate on domestic inflation becomes more widespread. The pass through from import prices into inflation is more rapid, and the result is that devaluation becomes less effective. Monetary sovereignty is therefore a diminishing benefit in a world where economies are becoming steadily more integrated and dependent on each other. This is a lesson that the small economies learned many years ago. But it is increasingly true of the medium-sized European economies as well. To sum up, therefore, the devaluation option can be useful in extreme circumstances. But it can also prove to be a temptation which is overused, and which can lead to more problems than it solves.

It is easy to overstate the usefulness of devaluation even in extreme circumstances when there is substantial unemployment (as there was in Britain in 1992, for example). Professor Niels Thygesen has pointed out that the size of the real devaluation (after allowing for offsetting rises in domestic prices) needed to cut unemployment by 1 percentage point is surprisingly large. Typically, computer models of medium-sized European economies estimate that exports increase by about half as much as the fall in the real exchange rate over a two-to-three-year period. With exports worth about one-third of GDP this implies that it would take a 20 per cent real devaluation to produce an increase in output of about 3 per cent. Yet this is the sort of increase needed to cut unemployment by 1 percentage point.[73] Thygesen concludes that his calculation suggests 'that giving up the use of exchange-rate changes makes only a modest difference to the macroeconomic performance of the EU economies.'

THE ARGUMENTS FOR THE EURO

Labour markets and unemployment

Within monetary union the devaluation option is ruled out. So the only means of adjustment to changes in economic circumstances is through product, labour and capital markets. This essentially means labour markets, because businesses generally run down production or move elsewhere if their profitability is hit. So an adverse shock to the demand for products leads to the need for cost-cutting, which means cuts in the cost of labour (whether wages or jobs). Wages are businesses' biggest cost, and this effect is unavoidable. (Many business people question this, and say that wage costs are only a tiny part of their total costs. But they are not counting the wage element in the components and services that they purchase.)

The adjustment comes through labour markets. Either wage increases can respond quickly to unemployment, giving businesses an incentive to hire more labour, or the unemployed can move; in Norman Tebbit's phrase, the unemployed can 'get on their bikes'. In the United States labour mobility is much higher than in Europe. If a region becomes depressed or opportunities begin to wilt, people simply move to more prosperous and dynamic parts of the country. In Europe labour mobility is much lower than in the United States even within member countries, let alone between them with all the additional language problems that a cross-national move implies. A study which looked at net migration among the fifty states of the United States by comparison with the sixty-four regions of the European Union found that the average proportion of the population that moved each year in Europe was 0.2 per cent, compared with 0.7 per cent in the United States.[74] Americans are mainly, after all, Europeans with the travel gene. Europeans seem to like staying put, as was graphically illustrated recently by a genetic study which matched the DNA in a Cro-Magnon man's skeleton found in the Cheddar Gorge to a descendant teaching at the local primary school.

However, the Eurosceptics are wrong to argue that Americans' willingness to move region is a crucial way of making their monetary

union work. Americans do not mainly move around according to highs and lows in different regional economies, happily offsetting rises and falls in the unemployment rate. If so, there would be an ebb and flow in state populations. They move because many of them do not like the cold and the rain in the North-east and Midwest, preferring the sunshine of Florida, Texas and California. These movements of population are long-term shifts, and are not related to short-term movements in the business cycle. The four sunshine states of Arizona, California, Florida and Texas formed 7 per cent of the US population in 1900, 14 per cent in 1950 and 26 per cent in 2000.

So the principal means of adjustment in monetary unions (including the United States) is real wage flexibility. Do real wages (that is, wages after allowing for the price level) adjust? The rough answer in Europe, including Britain, is that the labour market does not adjust rapidly to changes. Because employees may resist accepting a cut in the real value of their wages – indeed, they resist even a slowdown in the real rise – the effect of shocks in Europe has often been to throw people out of work. If companies faced by the need to adjust to changes in their marketplace and become more competitive are unable to save labour costs through more moderate pay increases, they will save labour costs through employing fewer people instead. By comparison with the United States, Europe's growth has thus been employment-lean.

There is no easy way of comparing different labour-market institutions with a simple quantitative indicator for flexibility except the end result: the unemployed as a proportion of the labour force were 8 per cent in the European Union at the end of 2000 compared with 4 per cent in the United States.[75] Clearly, the labour market functions better in the United States. It would be wrong, however, to conclude from this comparison that Europe cannot afford to indulge in the luxury of monetary union. Indeed, if real wages are rigid (that is, if pay rises merely compensate for any increase in prices), then devaluation will be as useless an option as it is in monetary union. A country with rigid

real wages may as well benefit from the advantages of monetary union. There is no advantage in having a separate currency with the possibility of devaluation: any devaluation will raise import prices, and that will in turn cause an offsetting rise in wages. Real wages remain the same, and there is no benefit to competitiveness.

In fact, the picture is not as gloomy as many pretend. First, unemployment is high in Europe partly because the business cycle is lagging behind the United States. The unemployment rate peaked at 7.5 per cent in the United States in 1992, and fell steadily from then on. In the European Union, the peak was two years later at 11.1 per cent in 1994. The decline in Europe since then began in a very sluggish way, but has substantially accelerated since the launch of the euro at the beginning of 1999. The euro area unemployment rate has fallen by more than 1.5 percentage points in two years compared with a fall of only 1.1 percentage points in the previous four years. Moreover, employment growth since the launch of the euro has been twice as rapid in the euro area than in either Britain or the United States.

However, most economists agree that Europe's relatively high unemployment will not be cured by higher growth on its own. The main reason unemployment is higher is because of structural causes: higher unemployment benefits as a proportion of previous income; less intensive pressure on benefit claimants to search for work and accept jobs; more powerful trade unions when they do not co-ordinate their views; less ability to fire employees without compensation thereby making employers more cautious about hiring; and so on. These exist in Europe whether there is EMU or not. The existence of the devaluation option does not help, as we have discussed, because these same real wage rigidities which are held to be an impediment to EMU are also an impediment to the effectiveness of a devaluation. Labour-market rigidities, not the choice of monetary regime, are the principal cause of unemployment.

This point is borne out by a comparison of different European countries. Although it is true that the average level of unemployment

in Europe is much higher than in the United States, the most striking feature of European unemployment is not its high average level but the large differences between countries. As Professor Stephen Nickell has pointed out, European unemployment rates ranged from 1.8 per cent in Switzerland to 19.7 per cent in Spain if the post-recession period of 1983–96 is taken as a whole.[76] (This long period provides some guarantee against a distortion owing to different business cycle timings.) Unemployment was lower in Austria, Germany, Norway, Sweden and Switzerland than it was in the United States.[77] In fact, nearly one-third of developed Europe's population enjoyed average unemployment rates lower than those in the United States.

Professor Nickell makes another important point in the context of the debate about monetary union, which is that the conventional wisdom on labour-market rigidities is not always right. Some types of labour-market rigidities help promote an adjustment to an external shock. For example, countries where there is co-ordination between employers or employees or both may be able to react rationally to external shocks more effectively than a so-called flexible-market country. (This may be particularly effective in small countries where most of the key players can be brought together in one room.) Nickell points out that some of the European countries with the lowest unemployment rates (Austria, Switzerland, Germany, Sweden) are not known for their labour-market flexibility, whereas the more flexible Britain has had unemployment higher than half of its European neighbours.

Nickell concludes that high unemployment is associated with four principal factors: generous benefits that run on indefinitely without a stringent test of willingness to work; high unionisation and collective bargaining without co-ordination; high overall taxes impinging on labour combined with high minimum wages for young people; and poor educational standards at the bottom of the labour market. None of these are associated with the monetary regime. All are within the power of national governments to fix whether inside or outside EMU. And all will remain a problem whether inside or outside EMU.

Figure 4.1   **Decline from peak unemployment**
% of labour force (ILO definition) October–November 2000
compared with national peak

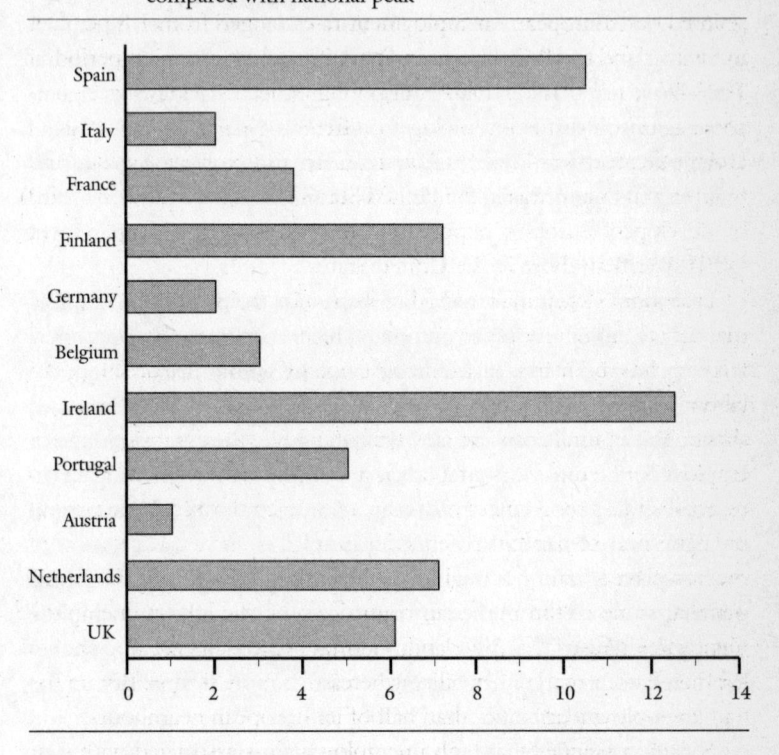

The good news, however, is that 'best practice' is gradually spreading around the European Union, and it is one of the reasons why the fall in unemployment has been accelerating. It is particularly encouraging that unemployment has dropped faster than might have been expected purely from the acceleration of European growth. As the Bank for International Settlements (BIS) – no cheerleader for anything – recently pointed out: 'The fact that unemployment can be reduced even when output growth is low suggests that progress has been made

in making labour markets more flexible and in reducing structural unemployment'.[78] The contrast between European unemployment today and its peak in the years after the two big oil shocks is notable in several countries. The bar chart shows the decline in the unemployment rate in euro area countries compared with the most recent peak. The chart clearly shows that Europe is gradually tackling its unemployment problem. Four euro area countries – Spain, Ireland, Finland and the Netherlands – have made particularly impressive progress, outstripping the performance of the United Kingdom.

Conversion costs

One undoubted cost of introducing the euro is the conversion of information technology systems, automatic teller machines and coin-operated machines. There is little reliable evidence within Britain about the extent of these costs. The Confederation of British Industry has said: 'Although the total costs are far from negligible, they are certainly not likely to be the most important aspect of signing up to the single currency even in purely economic terms. Transition costs (like transition savings) can be something of a distraction.'[79]

However, Britain has a national talent for making a meal of these matters, as we saw from the very much greater expenditure within the UK on the alleged Year 2000 computer bug whose ill effects nevertheless failed to materialise in countries like Italy that approached the whole matter with insouciance.[80] One estimate of the euro conversion costs commissioned by the anti-euro lobbying group Business for Sterling suggested a head-line grabbing £34.4 billion to £36.2 billion (or some 3.9 per cent to 4.1 per cent of GDP in 1999).[81] In fact, though, this figure is ludicrously high.

The calculations on which it is based are no better than back of the envelope jottings, and are often far bigger than more detailed calculations undertaken in particular sectors of the economy. For example, the Business for Sterling calculation projects that the cost to the banking sector would be £2.5 billion whereas the British Bankers' Association

itself estimates £1 billion. Similarly, the Business for Sterling study claims the cost to retailers as £3.5 to £5 billion. But the British Retail Consortium commissioned its own study suggesting that the costs would be £1.7 billion.[82] The Business for Sterling study was undertaken very quickly, as it was commissioned on 19 January 2000 and finalised on 11 February.

The most reliable guide to costs in Britain is to look at the costs being incurred on the Continent. The most authoritative estimate in Germany suggests that the total cost to the German economy will be 0.54 per cent of GDP, and that the payback will be identifiable annual savings of 0.22 per cent of GDP.[83] The Dutch central bank has estimated a similar outlay of 0.51 per cent of GDP, with a return of 0.25 per cent of GDP.[84] My own guess, based on the lack of concern about this issue on the continent, is that many of these supposed costs are absorbed in a businesses' normal re-investment programme as part of the constant process of upgrading. The Continental estimates of changeover costs are smaller than a fifth of the Business for Sterling numbers, and are based on real preparations on the ground rather than feverish imaginings. In both the Dutch and the German cases, the payback period is less than three years, a return that most businesses would regard with relish.

It is true, of course, that some companies will see only tangible costs but feel only intangible gains: for example, operators of gaming machines, vending machines and many small shopkeepers. However, all businesses would benefit from the extra growth that monetary union will bring, even if they are not direct beneficiaries because they are exporters. A rising tide floats all ships.

Summary

In this chapter we have looked at the often-cited disadvantages of EMU and some other problems that are not so well known. The removal of an independent monetary, interest-rate and exchange-rate policy will entail some loss of flexibility. However, we have seen that

the extent to which member countries' economies differ from each other is within the bounds seen in other monetary unions, including some European ones. The growing interdependence of the European economies also means that an independent monetary policy is becoming less useful, and we have seen that it is too optimistic to suppose that British monetary policy has always been used in a sensible and countercyclical manner. Indeed, it has itself been a source of important shocks to the economy, notably in 1974–6 and in 1979–81. Trade patterns in Britain are not much different from those in the euro area participants so there is no reason to expect particular shocks from that source. Also Britain's dependence on variable interest rates, a weakness arising from its inflationary history, does not make its economy more likely to react to interest-rate changes than those of existing euro area members.

Although the Stability and Growth Pact limiting deficits and debt is unnecessarily conservative, we have also seen that the present fiscal positions of the euro area members, and of Britain, are such that there is room to absorb the impact of a normal recession without breaching the guidelines. Fiscal policy is therefore more powerful as a potential stabilising force than it has been for a generation. Lastly, we have seen that Europe's unemployment rates vary widely depending on national labour-market institutions and not on the monetary regime. Those countries that suffer high unemployment and rigid labour markets would have problems inside or outside EMU. Indeed, for a devaluation to work for them they need to have labour markets which will accept that pay should not chase after prices. A devaluation, through the exercise of an independent monetary policy, therefore does not help their predicament.

5 The political consequences of EMU

In this chapter we look first at James Forder's fear that we would be delegating extraordinary powers to unelected officials if we were to join the euro. We then turn to the fear that the euro is merely a stalking horse for a much wider and deeper process of European integration. In effect, the euro is, in this view, a step towards a European superstate. Lastly, we look at some more likely results from the creation of the euro and the new realpolitik of a Europe largely controlled by centre-left governments in Britain, France, Germany and Italy for the first time since the Second World War.

Delegating powers to unelected officials

Part of the political compromise that created the euro was that the European Central Bank (ECB) should be modelled largely on the German Bundesbank, a central bank which had a track record second to none of controlling inflation during the post-war period. An essential element of the ECB's credibility with the financial markets is that it inherits the Bundesbank's mantle. It is independent of political pressures to set interest rates, and will therefore deliver low and stable inflation. This is why investors are prepared to lend money to governments participating in the euro at lower interest rates than they are to the United States of America.

Will we, though, be selling our democratic heritage? If so, it is surprising how many other countries have done this already, both inside and outside the group of euro participants. Indeed, Britain was the last country of the Group of Seven leading industrial economies to make its central bank independent when Gordon Brown, the Chancellor of the Exchequer, adopted Liberal Democrat policy after the

general election of 1997. Do we really believe that France, Germany, Italy, Canada, Japan or the United States were less democratic than Britain because they delegated powers to a specialised institution? Do we really think that Britain became fundamentally less democratic when Mr Brown handed the setting of interest rates to the Bank of England's Monetary Policy Committee? And what about the situation in Britain before 1946, when the Bank of England was nationalised? Were we less democratic then?

Our politicians have delegated many powers to institutions at one remove from political temptation, including the Arts Council, the British Broadcasting Corporation, National Health Service trusts, the Mersey Docks and Harbour Board, regional development agencies, the Docklands Development Corporation, and so on. The ECB is no different. Experience suggests that monetary policy is better conducted by people who do not have a direct interest in using it to secure their own re-election. Having an institution that is thoroughly credible in its anti-inflationary credentials even means that governments regain some power to use fiscal policy (taxation and spending) to cushion movements in their economies within the limits of the Maastricht Treaty. The lack of credibility of most European governments since their reactions to the 1973–4 and 1979–80 oil-price shocks has taken years to put right.

Indeed, it was precisely the inability of most politicians to respond rapidly to the need for higher interest rates in the early 1970s that created many of the problems in Europe today. Politicians were intrinsically too inclined to take the soft option with the result that inflation got out of hand, and the ultimate measures taken to control it were far more draconian and damaging to the economy than if a stitch had been taken in time. It is therefore perfectly possible to support central bank independence without believing in monetarism, despite James Forder's arguments, because experience shows that politically controlled interest rates are too slow to go up and too quick to come down. Independent central banks are simply designed to ensure that

the stitch in time saves nine. People who now argue that politicians should be given back control over interest rates appear to have forgotten the sad circumstances which led most informed people to conclude that politicians should not control interest rates.

Three models of central banking

Within the overall group of independent central banks there are three broad models. In the United States the Federal Reserve Board (Fed) is unique in that it is meant explicitly to take account of jobs as well as inflation. In Britain, Sweden and New Zealand the central banks are meant to look only at inflation, but the government sets the inflation target. In other central banks, including formerly all the continental European banks and now the ECB, the central bank itself is enjoined to aim at price stability. In the case of the ECB it has defined this as a range of inflation of 0–2 per cent.

There is much less to choose between these arrangements than some suggest because paper constitutions are only one influence on actual decisions. People matter, and so does the social environment. The Bundesbank has always been acutely aware of its political support in the country as any central bank must be. It has been able to take tough decisions because of the German folk memory of hyperinflation under the Weimar republic in the 1920s. This has certainly been of much more importance to the Bundesbank than its 'monetarism' as it repeatedly missed its monetary targets. That history of hyperinflation will be less of a consideration for the ECB because few other countries shared the experience. Indeed, if the ECB were seen to be acting in an irresponsibly restrictive manner, driving inflation down too far and too fast, it would soon have to respond to the arguments and pressures from business and the trade unions.

At the other end of the spectrum, the Fed should perhaps have been more relaxed than other central banks both because it is meant to consider the employment effects of its policies and because the States has never suffered a hyperinflation like Germany. But u

Volcker, the Fed pursued a tighter monetary policy against inflation in 1979 than almost any other central bank. So, once again, the paper constitution matters less than the people making the decisions and the context in which they work.

Far from being rigidly monetarist, the new ECB has adopted pragmatic monetary policy guidelines based on assessing a range of indicators and on monetary reference values. There are no formal money supply targets. The ECB has given regular evidence to the European Parliament on its policies and progress, and the parliament has pressed it to move beyond its relatively secretive Bundesbank inheritance. Although it does not publish the votes or minutes of the meetings – unlike the US Federal Open Market Committee or the Bank of England – it responded to the requests of the European Parliament both to publish regular economic forecasts and its econometric models. Overall, most market participants feel it has withstood the challenges of its first two years – a declining value of the euro against the dollar, and a rise in oil prices – rather well. Although the ECB raised interest rates, they remained relatively low in real terms, allowing the European recovery to become established. Inflation stayed low, and growth in the euro area in 2000 was the highest for ten years, as was the growth in jobs. This is simply inconsistent with the story that the ECB is a purblind, super-restrictive monetarist institution.

A cover for a superstate?

There is a second strand of concern about the euro, which is that it is a plot to drag us into a political union. Certainly, there are many people in Europe who actively want the process of integration to continue and deepen and for whom EMU is an important step. They hope that a single currency will provide a spur to greater integration. But they are not necessarily right. Whether the single currency entails further political consequences will be a matter for decision in an intergovernmental conference in 2004. But the omens are not good for the integrationists.

The Nice Treaty at the end of 2000 did not entail more centralising powers. Indeed, the nation states made it clear that they were not prepared to jettison their own interests. Several countries, such as France, that pay lip-service to greater integration in fact insisted on retaining more national vetoes even than Britain. Even Germany blocked the extension of majority voting in some areas, notably immigration. There was a modest extension of the areas to be agreed by majority voting (rather than unanimity), but the proportion of votes needed to establish a qualified majority went up. And Germany said that it wants to limit the powers of the European level of government when the next Treaty is decided in 2004. The limits of the 'ever closer union' first described in the Treaty of Rome will be set. As at Nice, Britain will have the absolute right to veto any changes to future treaties because any treaty amendment has to be ratified by each country. So in legal and constitutional terms it is incorrect to say that Maastricht will entail further integration.

Those concerned about any trend to a superstate usually over-estimate the power and influence of the EU institutions as they are today. The EU matters. It allows the member states to exercise public choices on environmental, consumer safety and other issues that they would not do otherwise. But the EU is not a superstate nor anything near one. The influence of a level of Government can be measured in three different ways: by what it spends, by how much it legislates and by who it employs. On all three measures, the European level of government is still very small. Spending by all levels of government in Europe takes 45 per cent of GDP, but the European level spends just 1.11 per cent of GDP. Moreover, the EU budget is declining as a share of national income, and has an absolute limit set by Treaty of 1.27 per cent of GDP. Although there was an increase in legislation at the end of the 1980s when the single market was established, the Council of Ministers and the European Parliament have been repealing as much legislation as they have put on the statute book over the last ten years. Overall, the stock of EU law has been roughly stable. Finally, the

number of employees of all the institutions in Brussels – the Commission, Council of Ministers and the European Parliament – is 23,000 people. This is half the number employed by the BBC, and less than half the 56,000 on the staff of Birmingham City Council.

The single currency may, of course, eventually set up political processes that will lead to more political decisions at the European level. If the single currency is perceived to be a great success, providing all the benefits outlined in Chapter 2 and more, much of the existing scepticism about European institutions may begin to erode. There may be more willingness to embark upon EU decision processes in other areas which are currently up to intergovernmental co-operation (such as foreign affairs and defence). But there is no direct or irrevocable link with greater political integration. However, the Eurosceptics do not generally argue that we should stay out of EMU because it will be successful. They say instead that EMU will fail. And if it fails in some spectacular manner there is little doubt that the debacle would cast a pall over all the European Union's institutions and would create serious doubts about the advisability of further integration. Far from hastening a European superstate, EMU would then have driven a nail into its coffin.

Many economists in the financial sector and academe have tried hard to envisage circumstances in which EMU might break up.[85] One scenario is an Italian political and financial crisis which leads to the wholesale flight of Italian money into German bank accounts and banknotes (ahead of the time when the euro becomes a physical reality in 2002), and which causes the Germans to reintroduce a separate monetary policy for fear of contagion. Given the large amount of short-term debt issued by Italy and Belgium (a short maturity which means that investors have to continue to make decisions to renew their investment, and which is therefore vulnerable to a shift in sentiment), this is not an outlandish prospect.

Nevertheless, these sorts of scenarios have generally lacked credibility with the financial markets. All three leading credit-rating agencies

regard the chances of such a break-up as small enough to warrant awarding the monetary union the coveted AAA status. The markets themselves increasingly price government securities of the euro members in line with differences in their debt and fiscal performance, ignoring currency and inflation-risk differences. As already noted, Italy has been able to borrow money more cheaply than the United States, a market judgement that does not suggest EMU is about to break down quickly.

A more tangible risk, which might have political consequences, is that the Maastricht architecture may need amendment because it is deemed to be inadequate. If EMU proves to create difficulties for some or several member states there will almost certainly be pressure for changes in procedures, and these could involve greater integration. The Treaty itself was the outcome of a laborious process of negotiation, which included many compromises, and in certain key respects it is already out of date. For example, it insists on a set of convergence criteria, including exchange-rate stability within the ERM, which looked sensible before the ERM crisis of 1992–3 but which now looks odd. We know that markets can attack currencies even if their fundamentals are strong and there is no need for devaluation – look at the attack on the French franc in 1993. It is precisely because of the difficulty of sustaining a fixed exchange rate in a world of free capital flows that the case for a single currency becomes even more compelling.

The most likely candidate for causing trouble is the Stability and Growth Pact (SGP) and the commitments in the Treaty itself to low deficits. These restrictions were introduced at German insistence to limit the possibility that large government deficits and debts might eventually set up a strong incentive for the monetary authorities to lend a member government money, and hence increase the money supply and inflation. The processes will certainly address this risk of political incontinence most effectively, but with the danger of introducing unnecessary limitations on the freedom of action of member states. These restrictions inevitably hamper a member state's ability to

use fiscal policy to stabilise its own economy if it is faced by a particularly large shock. Under the SGP a country has to seek the approval of the Council of Ministers if it is likely to run a deficit of more than 3 per cent of GDP unless GDP itself has fallen by 2 per cent. This rigidity may in turn mean that there will be greater pressure to deal with such shocks at a Europe-wide level rather than at the national level.[86] Ironically, Germany's insistence on measures designed to protect it from other countries' profligacy may entail new fiscal measures overall.

We have already seen, however, that all the euro area countries have steered their deficits to within the limits that would normally allow them to weather a recession without breaching the 3 per cent guideline, so this is unlikely to be a large problem. But it is hard in principle to see why a country with a low level of debt should not, if it wants, react to a particularly grave recession with an even more active fiscal policy, such as bringing forward infrastructure spending and cutting taxes. In other circumstances a country may have a large public capital programme to improve infrastructure, which might put in place assets counterbalancing any increased deficit. Yet the Maastricht Treaty prohibits even a country which has paid off all its national debt from running budget deficits of more than 3 per cent of GDP each year without the approval of the Council of Ministers. A sensible change would therefore be to allow governments with debt well within the 60 per cent of GDP limit to have greater flexibility to use fiscal policy as they see fit, and leave the markets to decide what the cost of funds should be. If a government is seen to have embarked on an irresponsible policy it will certainly pay a price in a high cost of funds when it borrows.

Member states may develop national solutions

It is also possible that member states may develop national rather than EU-wide means of absorbing shocks to their economy which will help to stabilise the Europe-wide economy. The use of fiscal policy (taxation and public spending) was originally advocated by John Maynard

Keynes as a way of encouraging more spending by consumers and businesses. But it may be possible to develop levers which have similar effects, and which bypass the fiscal process. For example, Finland has agreed, through its central labour market institutions, to set up two parallel EMU buffer funds for unemployment insurance and occupational pensions. Both received a slightly higher than necessary contribution during years of falling unemployment (starting in 1999) so that they build up a reserve. These reserves, totalling 2.5 per cent of the wage bill in the case of the pensions buffer fund, will then be run down in years of rising unemployment, thereby avoiding some rise in contributions.

Many European countries are now actively considering reforms of their old-age pension provision that would involve mandatory contributions to a personal retirement fund – in effect, compulsory savings. Most already have fiscal incentives for employees to save for their retirement. It would be a simple matter to ask a council of economic advisers to vary both the compulsory contributions and the incentives in line with the business cycle in each country. There would be higher contributions in booms when saving needs to be encouraged and lower ones in recessions when spending is in order. Such countercyclical measures would lack the political difficulties traditionally associated with the active use of fiscal policy, when higher public spending undertaken in slow years continues into fast ones, ratcheting up the scale of government. (This idea was adopted as Liberal Democrat policy in the autumn of 1998 as part of a series of proposals to prepare Britain for membership of EMU.)

Another interesting idea, put forward by Giles Keating of CS First Boston, an investment bank, is that countries might vary the capital requirements of their banks depending on the state of the business cycle. Capital, mainly shareholders' funds, is the cushion that banks have to use to pay depositors if loans turn bad. At present, banks have to keep a minimum amount of capital worth 8 per cent of their lending and other assets (such as government bonds). If there were a

particularly strong upswing under way which affected the prices of assets, such as property and shares, banks would have to have more of their own shareholders' funds to back a given amount of lending. This would recognise the increased future risks of such lending. But it would also make such lending less attractive to the bank, giving policy-makers another lever to influence overall spending in the economy. If there were a recession such capital adequacy ratios would be allowed to decline, enabling more lending for a given amount of capital. Since banking regulation remains a national responsibility within EMU, this could be introduced by any participating member.

If a government wanted to reintroduce a substantial measure to influence demand within its territory, despite being a member of the monetary union, it could even decide to levy a surtax on interest payments. At times of high demand growth, the surtax could help to build up a reserve fund which would be run down with a tax relief on interest payments at times of low demand growth. Such mechanisms, though, form no part of the normal armoury of a monetary union. In reality, the problems they are designed to address never seem serious enough to warrant the effort to introduce and run them.

It is true, of course, that many existing monetary unions tend to have a much more substantial degree of fiscal integration – of shared taxes and public spending – than the euro area. Eurosceptics worry that EMU will need a similarly expanded degree of support at the federal level. After all, the federal level of government in most federal states spends some 20–25 per cent of GDP, whereas the European Union budget in 2000 is 1.11 per cent of GDP and has to be kept within a Treaty limit of 1.27 per cent of GDP. As we have seen, much of the spending which would normally be undertaken by a federation is currently undertaken at national level in Europe. However, the often high spending by the central government in federations entails a surprisingly small amount of genuine insurance of one state by the federation. I have already cited the evidence that shows that the American system insures only about 10 cents in every dollar fall in state income, rather

than the 30 cents that some studies have suggested.[87] The study goes on to show that only a small amount of 'fiscal federalism' (a fiscal system at supranational level) might be necessary to achieve such a result if it was targeted as an insurance system. In general, federal spending provides many other public goods and services (such as, in the United States, the postal service and Medicare) which do not have the function of insurance.

This general conclusion – that there does not need to be a substantial amount of EU-level spending even if we want EU-level insurance – is in line with a major study on the same subject done for the European Commission under the chairmanship of Sir Donald Mac-Dougall.[88] The MacDougall committee, in line with the spirit of the times (1977) in which it reported, stressed the importance of having a constant redistribution from rich to poor regions rather than merely insuring against sudden shifts. Its scope therefore went well beyond what has been regarded as politically desirable in recent times. But even MacDougall concluded that, in order to achieve the redistributive effect of national budgets, the EU budget would need to rise to something of the order of 2–7 per cent of GDP (7.5–10 per cent of GDP if defence were included). In other words, a careful targeting of Community policies would leave the EU-wide level of government at only one-third the size of the federal levels of governments in Germany, Canada or the United States.[89]

These studies are important because they allay the fears of many Europeans that a superstate in Brussels will be a consequence of the single currency. In my view, it is likely that the existing framework of Maastricht will be adequate to the challenges it will face. Its inflexibilities might be dealt with by the development of new policy levers at national level, or by the further delegation of powers over fiscal policy to the national governments. This is by no means impossible. The Maastricht architecture is not written in stone and will certainly continue to develop. Moreover, the fiscal provisions should be easy to change, since the detailed provisions of the SGP form part of a

Council regulation rather than the Treaty itself and can therefore be changed by the Council of Ministers.

But even if this route is not chosen, and some EU-wide insurance system or even a permanently redistributive system as proposed by MacDougall is deemed necessary, the size of the EU budget would remain small as a proportion of income by comparison with the size of national member states' budgets. The European Union is already an incipient federation, in the sense that it elects to perform different public tasks at different levels of government, with some at European level, but it will always remain unique and is unlikely to follow the same path as other federations. The national government level will remain far, far stronger, even if the Maastricht architecture has to be amended as radically as the most pessimistic fear. There is no prospect of an EU superstate.

Tax harmonisation

Given some of the misconceptions about Maastricht, it is also worth pointing out that there are Treaty limits on public borrowing, but not on tax or public spending. Tax and spending is entirely up to the ideological and national preferences of the member states, and they vary widely. Indeed, the attempt by the Europhobes to suggest that Britain's adoption of the euro would require tax harmonisation is as misguided as it is mischievous. Within the present euro area member states, there is a substantial difference in the tax burden ranging from Ireland at 33 per cent of GDP to France at 50 per cent of GDP.[90] Nor is there any need in principle for tax harmonisation within a monetary union, as the experience of the United States shows. The individual states are free to levy whatever local taxes they want. New Jersey recently exempted clothing from sales tax, and caused the closure of all the skiwear shops in New York City. Vermont charges 7 cents in the dollar more income tax than next door New Hampshire (and 9.5 cents for higher rate taxpayers), but Vermont residents do not move because they think they get better public services.

Within the EU, the idea of countries competing to reduce sales taxes has seemed silly. So there are some common rules designed to make the single market function better and avoid losses of revenue to national exchequers. There is a directive setting minimum rates of both Value Added Tax and excise duties on tobacco and alcohol. But they are set at such a low level that British governments of both Conservative and Labour persuasion have sought to raise them (in order to stop the revenue losses from people buying cheaper cigarettes and tobacco in Belgium and France). There is a Code of Conduct under which member states promise not to tailor specific tax breaks to attract a company to set up in their country, in order to avoid a Dutch auction. But there is no proposal for a minimum corporation tax rate so long as countries apply the tax rates equally to all comers. Thus Ireland is levying a 12.5 per cent corporation tax rate which is very attractive to businesses.

Some people have proposed an EU-wide minimum level of withholding tax to ensure that savers cannot evade taxes by depositing money in Luxembourg or Austria. However, the Council of Ministers has instead agreed an approach whereby national tax authorities will exchange information on payments of interest and dividends. There is no proposal for, (and there would be no basis in the Treaties for) any harmonisation of income taxes or taxes in general. Indeed, Commissioner Frits Bolkestein, who is responsible for taxation and the single market, recently argued that there is a clear role for member states to compete in providing light taxation. EMU does not need, and will not entail, tax harmonisation.

International political consequences

Turning to international consequences, much will depend on the development of the euro as a reserve currency used by central banks to intervene in setting their own currency's level. The more important the euro becomes as an international asset, the greater the call will be for a collective European view. At present, the European role in helping to

resolve crises, such as the Mexican currency crash in December 1994 or the Asian crisis in the wake of the Thai baht devaluation in July 1997, is minimal. Several European governments, particularly the German government, were riled that the US Treasury unilaterally decided on the Mexican rescue package with minimal prior consultation. In Asia the Europeans were bit players. But Europe would certainly be expected to play a far more significant role if the euro internationalises quickly, a process that would be hastened by British membership. This in turn will put pressure on the euro area finance ministers to come to common positions on many of the big financial issues of the day. Indeed, this could be essential for financial stability. If the dollar's role is seriously weakened, the United States will be correspondingly less able to lead from the front in resolving financial crises.

Britain's membership of the euro would be likely to have another political consequence, as it would strengthen the more liberal and market-oriented forces within the group. Each participating member has, of course, both market-oriented and interventionist or dirigiste political forces. But, in general, the commitment to free trade, free capital flows and the exercise of restraint in any government intervention has been strongest in the northern countries: Austria, Britain, Denmark, Finland, Germany, Ireland, the Netherlands and Sweden. British membership, which would probably be accompanied soon after by Danish and Swedish membership, would tilt the balance decisively. The practical consequences could be felt across a wide range of issues. Indeed, Britain's exclusion from the first wave of entrants may already have had an influence by default on the ECB's operating procedures, notably the insistence on a mandatory cash-reserve requirement for banks and the conservative publication policy of the ECB.

6 **Options and conclusions**

The British, by temperament, prefer small and gradual changes. Over time these changes may build up, but there should be nothing too dramatic or revolutionary if we can help it. EMU was therefore everything that British policymakers usually dislike. It was a large, dramatic, discontinuous and radical change. Indeed, it has been the largest change in international monetary arrangements since the Bretton Woods system after the Second World War. It is arguably the largest single change in the framework of economic policy that has ever been tried in Europe, including Bretton Woods and the gold standard.

What is, however, incontrovertible is that monetary union has happened, and it has happened on a much larger scale than most British policymakers, let alone the Eurosceptics, ever believed possible. With eleven founding members now joined in 2001 by Greece, the euro area is a currency area of similar size to the United States, with a similar weight on the world economic stage. This fundamentally alters the status quo. Until 1 January 1999, the pound was just another European currency among many. But now it is a comparatively small currency set against a vast one, the movements of which completely dominate the inflationary impact of import prices and the competitiveness of British exporters. The potential for great volatility in sterling has increased, particularly since the relationship between the euro and the dollar is itself likely to be more volatile as their respective monetary authorities care little about their exchange rates (since they affect only a small part of their now continent-wide economies). Given that international capital flows are also increasing inexorably – a trend that is likely to continue with the growth of private pensions – the potential for the pound to be squeezed between the great tectonic plates of

Europe and America has never been greater. It will not be comfortable.

In this context Britain cannot merely opt out and pretend that nothing is happening. If we are to stay out of the euro we must expect an even bumpier ride than we have had over the last twenty-five years of a largely floating exchange rate for sterling. We will need to reinforce the credibility of our monetary institutions, which will otherwise bear unfavourable comparison with those of the United States and the euro area.[91] We will also have to ensure that fiscal policy remains on track, as the cost of market punishment will be greater outside the euro than inside it. Not only can bond yields rise if the markets disapprove of a government's policy, but the exchange rate can fall. Moreover, the exchange rate may well come under strain because of developments in either the United States or euro area and require offsetting fiscal and interest-rate changes to compensate. After all, the Deutschmark/pound exchange rate dropped to just DEM2.2 in 1995 and went into overdrive in 2000 hitting DM3.45, helping to cause more than a third of a million unnecessary job losses among manufacturers.

The balance of costs and benefits points to British entry. The costs are often overstated. The divergences that have in the past occurred among the European economies – the problem that a one-size-fits-all monetary policy is meant to aggravate – have already been experienced in other monetary unions, notably the United States but also existing European countries. An independent monetary policy (both interest rates and exchange rate) is a diminishing asset in a world which is becoming increasingly interdependent. Moreover, it is wrong to assume that the freedoms an independent policy affords are unalloyed benefits. Many of the greatest shocks administered to the British economy over the post-war period have been home-grown instances of ill-judged policy, including far greater and more sudden shocks to our trading sectors (such as manufacturing in 1979–81) than are imaginable in EMU. The lack of an independent exchange rate and interest rate will put pressure on the remaining means of adjustment – the labour market – but this is already more flexible than it was, and

Britain is certainly as well able to adjust as other large EMU participants. We have also seen that Britain's economy is not disproportionately affected by short-term interest rates, despite the importance of
variable-rate mortgages.

On the benefits side, British adoption of the euro will improve
growth and jobs by two principal means: it will increase efficiency and
reduce risks. Consumers will have more choice and greater ease in
comparing prices. Competitive pressures will increase and so will efficiency. This is perhaps the most fundamental step forward, albeit often
underestimated by our macroeconomically obsessed policymakers.
The euro is already making a reality of the single European market and
providing businesses with opportunities for economies of scale of
which they could until recently only dream. The single market is
increasing prospective returns on investment, and thereby growth and
jobs. There will also be an elimination of the transactions costs in
moving from the pound to the euro. Britain can and should participate
in these gains.

The second mechanism by which EMU delivers important benefits
is through the reduction of risks, particularly exchange-rate uncertainty. This may be expected to boost trade flows, but, even more crucially, it is already boosting investment across borders within EMU and
raising the long-run growth rate of the European Union. By creating a
monetary area that is a continent-wide economy, EMU has insulated
its member economies from external shocks caused either by problems
in other economies or by financial flows and misaligned exchange
rates. Britain's membership would lift the constraint which British policymakers have often felt: the need to ensure that the balance of payments (of exports and imports) does not go too far into deficit. Within
EMU the balance of payments can no longer have a traumatic effect on
the exchange rate of an individual member state, or on its inflation
rate.

EMU also reduces the risks of inflation, and hence cuts intere
costs in the long run. The credibility of Europe's monetary ins

is already greater, as we have seen, than that of its American counter-parts. Governments whose countries are participating in the euro area are already able to borrow on better terms over a ten-year period than the American government, owing to the markets' belief that inflation is less likely to erode the value of the debt. If Britain joined, borrowers would also benefit from the reduction in interest costs, which could be £38 a month for the average mortgage payer over the business cycle.

Most importantly for our longer-term prospects, businesses should find capital more easily and cheaply just as our euro area competitors are doing now. Banks will compete fiercely for new business, and the new capital markets of the euro area are encouraging the growth of risk capital, particularly in the bond market. These interest rates and financial-market effects will help to reduce the cost of capital in Britain, and therefore boost investment. Lastly, the advent of a new world currency will offer all Europeans the advantage of seignorage: the ability to buy other people's exports and offer them printed banknotes in exchange. The euro is likely to become a major world currency, used as a store of value, a means of exchange and a unit of account much beyond the euro area.

These general advantages are reinforced by two particular features of Britain's situation, which mean that we may disproportionately benefit from the single currency. The first is our ability to attract foreign direct investment (FDI). If we join this will be underpinned. Indeed, we may benefit from the new wave of investment likely in the early years of EMU. The second is the position of the City of London as Europe's incipient financial centre. Within EMU London can be more than just a centre of international finance. It can be the centre of the new, integrated euro capital markets. Outside EMU not only is our share of FDI likely to dwindle, at particular cost to some of our poorer regions, but also the City's role is likely to come under increasing challenge from Paris and Frankfurt.

These unique British factors, the importance of FDI and of the City, are part of the answer to the questions: Why not wait and see how

things turn out? Delay always sounds reasonable. EMU has gone ahead with a large membership. The great experiment has begun. If we wait we also increase the risk of losses because foreign investors go elsewhere, and because other centres pick up business from the City. Nor are we likely to settle the issue by waiting. The sorts of things that might go wrong with EMU, as we have seen, are unlikely to happen quickly. They might never happen. They might happen only after twenty years. No one is really suggesting that we can wait that long. Even the 'doctrine of unripe time', that famous bureaucratic delaying tactic when arguments of principle fail or prove inexpedient, would not sustain British non-membership for such a period. The government is rightly worried about the loss of political influence within Europe entailed by Britain's non-membership in such an important European project.

There is another point about delay. If something creates serious strains within EMU the odds are that it will be fixed. The show will go on. This is the experience of the European Union to date, particularly with big projects such as EMU in which so much political capital has been invested. If we are out, we will not have the problems. But we will not be part of the solutions either. This will bring potential economic and political costs as well. Indeed, even a temporary delay could be used against Britain, as the delay in our initial membership of the European Union was used to put in place policies for agriculture and fisheries which were inimical to British interests. There is even a risk that Britain, outside EMU, could be 'de Gaulled' again while Paris and Frankfurt benefit at the expense of the City, and the Pas de Calais benefits at the expense of South Wales and the North-west in the race for Japanese and American investment. Far from being at the heart of European affairs, we could become as uncomfortably marginal as we felt in the 1960s. As Professor Willem Buiter, a former member of the Bank of England's Monetary Policy Committee, has said, 'Until the United Kingdom is a member of EMU, it will have second fiddle status in the concert of Europe.'

If you believe, as most British people seem to believe according to the opinion polls, that British membership of the euro is merely a matter of time, then it is supremely irrational to delay. We will, when we join, have to pay all the upfront costs (such as conversion costs for slot machines) in any case. But with each month that passes we are delaying the benefits. If an investment is worth undertaking, it is worth undertaking as soon as possible so as to bring the benefits on stream. British membership of EMU is precisely such a case. We will make the investment before long, so it makes no sense to delay the benefits. Nor does it make any sense to risk increasing the costs by prolonging our self-imposed period of political impotence. Time and again Britain has delayed participation in Europe-wide projects which our partners have deemed to be essential. We continue to pay the price for these delays in both the Common Agricultural Policy and the Common Fisheries Policy. How long must we go on doing so on this occasion?

The Eurosceptics increasingly recognise the power of this logic as they flail to find an alternative vision for Britain and its economy in the twenty-first century. This is one reason Conrad Black, the Canadian proprietor of the *Telegraph* newspapers, wrote an interesting article in his own journal, entitled 'Britain's final choice: Europe or America?', which rather let the cat out of the bag.[92] Mr Black argued that Britain should leave the European Union and become a member of the North American Free Trade Agreement (NAFTA). 'If the United States received a signal from a British government that it wished to avail itself of a North American option, they would respond immediately,' he wrote. 'If America were jubilant, Canada would be ecstatic.' So there is a secret agenda, but is not on the part of the pro-Europeans; it is the secret agenda of the anti-Europeans, which is to leave the European Union.

This is, of course, a rich newspaper proprietor's whimsy since the Americans have pushed hardest for British membership of the European Union, and take British views seriously in exact proportion to our influence in Europe.[93] For free traders, there is a good argument for trying to negotiate an Atlantic Free Trade Area (AFTA) including both

the EU and NAFTA.[94] But the argument that we should abandon the EU to join NAFTA is extraordinary. The cost of shipping a 40 foot cube container from Canterbury to the nearest port on the European mainland, Calais, is £450 whereas the cost of the same shipment to Boston, the nearest port in the US, is £1,540. Transport costs between Britain and NAFTA are three times as high as transport costs between Britain and the EU, and these costs dwarf tariffs. Inevitably, we will have a much closer trading relationship with our European partners than with the North Americans. Since we export nearly three times as much to the EU as to NAFTA, we would end up paying far more tariffs on EU exports than we would save on NAFTA exports particularly since two thirds of our trade with NAFTA is tariff free in any case. The amount of competition for the consumers' pound would be reduced, and we would give a whole new meaning to 'rip off Britain'.

The idea that leaving the European Union would allow us to regain control over our own concerns is also absurd. It completely fails to understand the globalised world in which we live. Norway is outside the EU, but its businesses need to sell in the EU, which is their largest market. As a result, Norway has introduced 3,000 items of EU legislation covering industrial standards, consumer safety requirements and environmental measures needed to ensure that its products comply with EU rules, and can have unfettered access to the single market. Yet the Norwegians have no influence over any of these rules in either the Council of Ministers or the European Parliament, because Norwegians are not represented. If that is what our Europhobes mean by national sovereignty, they should think again. We should never exchange the illusion of sovereignty outside the EU for the reality of power within it.

Leaving aside the question of geography, or perhaps oceanography, the problem for most British people with Mr Black's vision is that we have no more desire to become an appendage of the United States than to be subsumed into a European superstate. Yet recently a legal case brought by the US-based Ethyl Corporation under the NAFTA rules caused the Canadian Parliament to repeal a law designed to protect its

environment. There are six other similar cases. The European Union, which celebrates its cultural, social and ethnic diversity, suits British interests well. Most people realise that the threat to Britain's cultural identity does not come from Brussels, but from our seductive cousins across the Atlantic with their all-conquering Hollywood dream factory. British social values are more European than American, as is reflected in our relatively strong commitment to a welfare state and to relatively high provision of public services. Most British people know that there is no conflict between being British, English and a Yorkshire person. To be European is just another layer of our identity.

We cannot long stand aside from the central project of the European Union, already adopted by thirteen other member states and soon to be adopted as a matter of course by the thirteen candidate members in central and eastern Europe. The euro is a big change, but it has come to seem a much smaller one in the context of present hyperactive international markets. Do we want to live in a world where exchange rates can be so buffeted by speculation that they can move by nearly 10 per cent in one trading session, and where the reasonable expectations of our exporters can be overturned in a week? Lord Keynes warned that the financial system should never allow the bubbles and froth of speculation to undermine the steady efforts of commerce and industry. He was right. We need to use our sovereignty to provide a stable environment for our businesses, in the same way that we have rightly used our sovereignty to provide a secure defence within NATO. What sort of freedom is it to hike interest rates so high to defend your exchange rate that you drive the economy into recession? What sort of freedom is it to float your exchange rate and price hundreds of thousands out of work? Our present financial system is not sustainable. We can move back to a world where free movement of capital and even of trade come increasingly into question. Or we can ensure the benefits of greater international integration by adopting the euro. In a real world of hard choices, the pound's days are numbered. The euro is our future.

Notes

1   See 'Britain's adoption of the euro; report of the expert commission' chaired by the author, published in September 2000, which sets out a practical list of steps to enable UK adoption of the euro together with a timetable. It is available from www.chrishuhnemep.org or www.libdems.org

2   Available on HM Treasury website: www.hm-treasury.gov.uk/pub/html/docs/emumem/main.html

3   The average annual growth rate of GDP per head in the United Kingdom from 1960 to 1973 was 2.5 per cent against 3.7 per cent in Germany, 4.3 per cent in Italy and 4.5 per cent in France.

4   See Giavazzi and Giovannini (1989) for an analysis of exchange rate policy in Europe, including the formation of the European Monetary System.

5   Several academics made the argument, and so did the EU Commission in 'One market, one money'. Some economic commentators had also pointed out this problem, including me in an article in the *Independent* shortly before the break up.

6   Mergers and acquisitions figures were compiled by the equity strategy team at Morgan Stanley Dean Witter from Thomson Financial Securities data, and were kindly supplied to the author. This figure is the broad definition list the enterprise value of the target in all deals where there was a European company as either acquiror or target.

7   See Nam-Hoon Kang and Sara Johansson 'Cross-border Mergers and Acquisitions: Their Role in Industrial Globalisation', STI Working Papers 2000/1, OECD, Paris, 2000.

8   Calculations from the research department of the Bank of Tokyo-Mitsubishi supplied to the author.

9   At the end of November 2000, the Italian ten-year bond yield was just 5.3 per cent whereas the US Treasury was paying 5.45 per cent.

10 There were 120,619,000 jobs in the euro area economies in November 1998, and 125,361,000 in August 2000, according to Eurostat.

11 BEUC; Bureau Europeén des Unions de Consommateurs, 'Transferts de l'argent a l'intérieur de la CEE' April 1988.

12 EU Commission 'One Market, One Money' European Economy 44, Luxembourg, October 1990.

13 Engel and Rogers (1996).

14 Various Eurosceptics, including the Business for Sterling campaign, have suggested that this and other studies are not relevant because they were done before the North American Free Trade Agreement, which came into force in 1994, had full effect. However, the Canada–US free trade agreement began in 1990, and Engel and Rogers note in their article: 'If trade barriers are an important reason why the border variable is economically significant, one would expect that the magnitude of this variable would decline after 1989. In fact, we found a slight tendency in the opposite direction: the estimate border coefficients were usually larger in the post-1989 period.'

15 Computed by Fitch Ratings from data supplied by Capital Data Bondware.

16 Figures from the European Venture Capital Association.

17 Baldwin (1990). In the context of the European Union's single market 1992 programme, Baldwin estimated that the 'medium run growth bonus' might be half as much as the initial efficiency gains for Britain. With initial efficiency gains worth a minimum of 0.2 per cent of GDP through savings in transaction costs, this would imply a further 0.1 per cent a year growth bonus. See Emerson and Huhne for a discussion of these effects.

18 EU Commission, 'One Market, One Money'.

19 See Thygesen (1998) and Gros and Thygesen (1998).

20 J. McCallum, 'National borders matter: Canada–US regional trade

patterns', *American Economic Review*, 85.3, pp 615–23, June 1995.
This was confirmed in J. F. Helliwell, 'Do national borders matter for
Quebec's trade?', *Canadian Journal of Economics*, 1996.

21 Andrew K. Rose, 'One money, one market: the effect of common
    currencies on trade', *Economic Policy*, 30, April 2000. The results of
    this study are surprisingly robust, but the sample of monetary unions
    tends to be of relatively small countries or territories linked to bigger
    ones which may limit the applicability to Europe's monetary union.

22 'Europe's preparedness for EMU', Research Report 1997, KPMG
    Management Consulting.

23 This point relies heavily on Richard Baldwin (1989 and 1990).

24 See European Economy supplement A, no. 10/11, November 2000,
    European Commission Directorate-General for Economic and
    Financial Affairs, page 38.

25 The Council of Mortgage Lenders estimates that the average
    outstanding mortage at June 2000 was £46,000. The average new
    advance, however, is much higher at £59,779 for first time buyers
    and £79,646 for subsequent purchases.

26 For example, the comparable inflation measure – on the EU
    harmonised index of consumer prices – was 1 per cent over the year
    to October 2000 in the UK, compared with 2.7 per cent in the euro
    area. That means that real short-term interest rates, actual interest
    rates deflated by price rises, were 5 per cent in Britain against 2.2 per
    cent in the euro area. This might reflect cyclical considerations, but
    that would not explain the fact that the British government paid a real
    4 per cent against the German government's 2.2 per cent. In
    principle, these long-term real interest rates ought to equalise across
    the world after allowing for different risks.

27 EU Commission: 'One market, one money', 1990.

28 Earnings of men and women at full-time adult rates in April 2000
    were £21,842 according to the New Earnings Survey.

29 See Porter and Judson (1996).

30 This is the broadest measure of financial and business services, the so-

called FIREB sector which includes financial intermediation (banks and investment banks), real estate and letting, and business services (accountancy, consulting etc).

31 FDI is where the stake in the company is more than 10 per cent, generally held to be the point at which the investment ceases to be merely a part of a portfolio of shares that can be bought and sold without commitment.

32 Andersen Consulting (1998), from UNCTAD data.

33 JETRO data. On a ratio of the share of FDI to the share of GDP in the EU total, Britain outperforms all the larger member states and is exceeded only by Belgium, Sweden and the Netherlands.

34 Andersen Consulting (1998), from Eurostat.

35 Centre for Economic and Business Research (1992).

36 See Andersen Consulting (1998), page 22.

37 See Szymanski (1994).

38 These figures are drawn from the study conducted by the Centre for Economic and Business Research (1998) for the Corporation of London.

39 Ibid.

40 Ibid.

41 See Bank for International Settlements, Annual Report, 1998, Basle, page 84.

42 The Parliament needs an absolute majority of its members – 314 votes out of 627 – to amend a Council common position after first reading. If it does so, and both houses disagree, then there is a conciliation procedure in an attempt to reach a compromise.

43 See, for example, John Redwood (1997).

44 United Kingdom Balance of Payments, The Pink Book, 2000 edition, derived from Table 9.3.

45 Quoted by the Social Security Committee of the House of Commons, October 1996.

46 For the more financially sophisticated, the calculation is of the net present value of all future pension liabilities minus the net present

value of future contributions.

47 See 'Coping with the Ageing Problem' in OECD Economic Surveys 'Italy' May 2000, pages 99 – 113.

48 See 'Pension reform in France', Merrill Lynch, 12 April 2000.

49 See progress report to the Ecofin council on the impact of ageing populations on public pension systems, Economic Policy Committee, EPC/ECFIN/581/00-EN-Rev.1, Brussels, 6 November 2000, page 37.

50 A useful discussion of these issues is found in Arrowsmith, Barrell and Taylor (1998).

51 Mundell (1998).

52 Zenon G. Kontolemis and Hossein Samiei 'The UK business cycle, monetary policy and EMU entry'; International Monetary Fund Working Paper WP/00/210.

53 IMF (1997).

54 In the United Kingdom's case, the correlation coefficient with Germany was 0.19 while the Rocky Mountains' correlation coefficient with the Mid-east was 0.18.

55 Patrick Minford in the *Daily Telegraph*, 21 August 2000: 'Ireland's race against inflation can't be won with the euro'.

56 The EU measure of Irish consumer price inflation dropped from a peak of 6 per cent in November 2000 to 4.6 per cent in December and 3.9 per cent in January 2001.

57 See Balassa (1964) and Samuelson (1964).

58 European Central Bank Monthly Bulletin, October 1999, pages 36–44.

59 See Fatas (1998).

60 See Hummels, Rapoport and Yi (1998). Their study shows that such intra-industry or vertical trade was slightly higher in Britain, at 19.1 per cent of total trade, than in Germany (at 16.3 per cent) or France (at 18.7 per cent). All the European economies were much more vertically integrated than the United States (7.4 per cent) or Japan (6.6 per cent). In all cases vertical trade had been increasing sharply.

61 IMF Direction of Trade Statistics (merchandise trade) for 1999.

62 Both exports to the euro area and the non-euro countries have fallen back as a share of GDP in 1999, because of the rise in sterling.

63 Bank for International Settlements cited in Dornbusch, Favero and Giavazzi (1998).

64 See Ramaswamy and Sloek (1997).

65 Dornbusch, Favero and Giavazzi (1998). Previous studies assumed that interest-rate changes would affect the individual European economies as they have done in the past, including any effect on their exchange rates relative to other European countries. In EMU, of course, the interest rate will not affect the exchange rate with other EMU participants.

66 See Sachs and Sala-I-Martin (1992), who estimated 30–40 per cent of the original fall in income is compensated; Bayoumi and Masson (1996) estimate a net effect of 30 per cent.

67 See Fatas (1998). This result is also similar to Von Hagen (1992).

68 Fatas (1998).

69 The Stability and Growth Pact is set out in Council Regulations 1466/97 and 1467/97.

70 These are equivalent to 0.2 per cent of GDP plus a variable component of one-tenth of the difference between the deficit and 3 per cent of GDP up to 0.5 per cent of GDP.

71 This broad conclusion is supported by all the studies on this subject known to the author, including the IMF's usual structural budget balance measures. A different methodology used by researchers at the Austrian National Bank comes to the same conclusion. See Brandner, Diepalek and Schuberth (1998). The most recent estimates of the cyclical safety margin by the EU Commission were in Public Finances in EMU, 2000, a report of D.G. Ecofin in May 2000.

72 Currie (1997).

73 Thygesen (1998).

74 Emerson and Huhne (1991).

75 A recent paper which sets out research on real wage rigidity shows

that even the rank order of countries in terms of rigidity differs substantially according to the economic model chosen. See Vinals and Jimeno (1996). See also the estimates in Layard, Nickell and Jackman (1991).

76 Nickell (1997).

77 There is a useful discussion of the key features of the 'Rhineland' model in Davidson (1998).

78 Bank for International Settlements, Annual Report, 2000.

79 Appendix 12, Memorandum submitted by the Confederation of British Industry, in the Fourteenth report of the Trade and Industry Committee of the House of Commons, session 1999-2000, 'What would the euro cost UK business?', HC755.

80 The consulting firm Cap Gemini estimated that Britain spent $51 billion on the millenium bug problem, or 3.85 per cent of GDP. This compared with 1.25 per cent of GDP in Italy, 0.9 per cent of GDP in France and 2.3 per cent of GDP in the Netherlands.

81 Study prepared by Chantrey Vellacott, an accountancy firm, for Business for Sterling and available on www.bfors.com. An executive summary is cited in the Trade and Industry Committee report, op cit.

82 Memorandum submitted by the British Retail Consortium, citing its study by Abberton Associates, in the Trade and Industry Committee report, op cit.

83 Clemens, R; Icks, A. and Menke, A. (1998) 'Euro und Mittelstand – Neue Dimensionen auf internationalen Markten' Schriften zur Mittelstandsforschung Nr. 78 NF, Institut fur Mittelstandforschung, Bonn. http://www.ifm-bonn.org/ergebnis/78nf.htm

84 Prast, H. M and Stokman, A. C. J (1999) 'De euro in Nederland: uitkomsten van de achtste DNB-euro-enquete', (The euro in the Netherlands: results of the eighth DNB euro survey), Onderzoeksrapport WO&E nr. 580/9913, De Nederlandsche Bank NV, Amsterdam http://www.dnb.nl/research/woe/pdf/580.pdf

85 See for example Arrowsmith ed. (1998).

86 See for example Eichengreen and Wyplosz (1998).

87 Fatas (1998).

88 Commission of the European Communities (1977).

89 See also Sir Donald MacDougall's subsequent discussion of the study group; MacDougall (1992).

90 OECD Economic Outlook, November 2000, estimates for 2000, Annexe table 29 on General Government tax and non-tax receipts.

91 For a clear assessment of the options, including what needs to happen if we stay out of the euro, see the report of an independent panel chaired by Rupert Pennant-Rea, CEPR (1997).

92 Extracts from 'Britain's final choice: Europe or America?', a speech by Conrad Black at the annual meeting of the Centre for Policy Studies, *Daily Telegraph*, 10 July 1998.

93 As the former US ambassador to Britain, Mr Raymond Seitz, has said: 'If Britain's voice is less influential in Paris or Bonn, it is likely to be less influential in Washington.'

94 AFTA would make sense particularly since the residual tariffs are no longer very high following successive trade liberalisation rounds. The EU common external tariff averages 4.9 per cent while the US tariff averages 3.2 per cent.

References

Alberola, E. and Tyrvainen, T. (1998) 'Is there scope for inflation differentials in EMU? An empirical evaluation of the Balassa-Samuelson model in EMU countries', Discussion Papers, 15, Economics Department, Bank of Finland.

Andersen Consulting (1998) *Business, Britain and Europe: the first 25 years*, European Movement, London.

Arrowsmith, J. (1998, July) 'Large scale EMU: the May council decisions and implications for monetary policy', *National Institute Economic Review*, London.

Arrowsmith, J. (ed.) (1998) 'Thinking the unthinkable about EMU: coping with turbulence between 1998 and 2002', National Institute Occasional Paper No. 51, London.

Arrowsmith, J., Barrell, R. and Taylor, C. (1998, October) 'Managing the Euro in a Tri-polar World', paper presented at the 21st colloquium of the Société Universitaire Européene de Recherches Financières, Frankfurt (mimeo).

Balassa, B. (1964, December) 'The Purchasing Power Parity doctrine: a reappraisal', *Journal of Political Economy*.

Baldwin, R. (1989, October) 'The growth effects of 1992', *Economic Policy*.

Baldwin, R. (1990) 'On the microeconomics of EMU', in Commission of the European Communities, *One Market, One Money*.

Bayoumi, T. (1989, August), 'Saving Investment correlations: immobile capital, government policy or endogenous behaviour?', IMF Working Paper No. 89/66.

Bayoumi, T. and Masson, P. R. (1996) 'Fiscal flows in the United

States and Canada: Lessons for monetary union in Europe', *European Economic Review*.

Brandner, P., Diepalek, L. and Schuberth, H. (1998) 'Structural budget deficits and sustainability of fiscal positions in the European Union', Working Paper No. 26, Oesterreichische NationalBank, Vienna.

Bureau Européen des Unions de Consommateurs (BEUC) (April, 1988) *Transferts de l'Argent a l'intérieur de la CEE*.

Canzoneri, M., Diba, B. and Eudey, G. (1996, June) 'Trends in European productivity and real exchange rates: implications for the Maastricht convergence criteria and for inflation targets after EMU', Centre for Economic Policy Research, Discussion Paper No. 1417.

Centre for Economics and Business Research for the Confederation of British Industry (1992) *The impact of UK attitudes to the EU on inward investment into the UK*.

Centre for Economics and Business Research for the Corporation of London (1998) *The City's Importance to the European Union Economy*.

Commission of the European Communities (1977, April) *Report of the Study Group on the role of Public Finance in European Integration* (The MacDougall report), Brussels.

Currie, D. (1997) *The pros and cons of EMU*, Economist Intelligence Unit, London.

Davidson, I. (1998) *Jobs and the Rhineland Model*, Federal Trust.

Deutsch, R. (1998, January) *The advent of a true euro corporate and high yield market*, Merrill Lynch.

Dornbusch, R., Favero, C. and Giavazzi, F. (1998, April) 'Immediate challenges for the European Central Bank', *Economic Policy*, No. 26.

Eichengreen, B. (1996, December) 'EMU: an outsider's perspective', Center for International and Development Economics Research (CIDER), Working Paper No. C96-079, University of California, Berkeley.

Eichengreen, B. and Wyplosz, C. (1998, April) 'The Stability Pact: more than a minor nuisance?', *Economic Policy*.

Emerson, M. and Huhne, C. (1991) *The Ecu report*, London.

Emerson, M., Aujean, M., Catinat, M., Goybet P. and Jacquemin A. (1988) *The Economics of 1992*, OUP, Oxford.

Emerson, M., Gros, C., Italianer A., Pisani-Ferry J. and Reichenbach H. (1992) *One Market, One Money*, OUP, Oxford.

Engel, C. and Rogers, J.H. (1996, December) 'How wide is the border?', *American Economic Review*.

European Commission (1990, October) 'One Market, One Money', *European Economy*, No. 44, Luxembourg.

European Commission (1998) *Infeuro Newsletter*, No. 8.

Fatas, A. (1998, April) 'Does EMU need a fiscal federation?', INSEAD Working Paper, *Economic Policy*, No. 26.

Fatas, A. (1997, January) 'EMU countries or regions? Lessons from the EMS experience', *European Economic Review*, Vol. 41.

Feldstein, M. (1977) *Foreign Affairs,* Vol. 76, No. 6, pages 60–73.

Flora, P., Kraus, F. and Pfenning, W. (1987) *State, Economy and Society in Western Europe, 1815–1975*, two volumes, London.

Forder, J. (1998a) 'The case for an independent European Central Bank: A reassessment of evidence and sources', *European Journal of Political Economy*, Vol. 14, pages 53–72.

Forder, J. (1998b) 'Central Bank Independence – Conceptual Clarifications and Interim Assessment', *Oxford Economic Papers*, Vol. 50, pages 307–334.

Forder, J. (1998c) 'Is the European Union really a Friend of Free Trade?', Politeia Lecture, December 15th 1998.

Friedman, M. (1968) 'The role of monetary policy', *American Economic Review*, pages 1–17.

Giavazzi, F. and Giovannini, A. (1989) *Limiting exchange rate flexibility: the European Monetary System*, MIT press, Cambridge, MA.

Gros, D. and Thygesen, N. (1991) *European Monetary Integration*, Longman, London.

Gros, D. and Thygesen, N. (1998) *European Monetary Integration: From the EMS to EMU*, London and New York.

Hummels, D., Rapoport, D. and Yi, Kei-Mu (1998, June) 'Vertical specialisation and the changing nature of world trade', *Economic Policy Review*, Vol. 4, No. 2, Federal Reserve Bank of New York.

IMF (1997, October) *World Economic Outlook*.

Johnson, C. (1996) *In with the Euro, out with the pound: the single currency for Britain*, London.

KPMG Management Consulting (1997) 'Europe's preparedness for EMU', Research Report.

Layard, R., Nickell, S. and Jackman, R. (1991) *Unemployment: macroeconomic performance and the labour market*, Oxford.

MacDougall, Sir D. (1992, May) 'Economic and Monetary Union and the European Community budget', *National Institute Economic Review*, National Institute of Economic and Social Research.

Mazower, M. (1998) *Dark Continent: Europe's twentieth century*, London.

Milesi, G. (1998) *Le Roman de l'Euro*, Paris.

Mundell, R. (1998, 24 March) 'Great Expectations for the Euro', *Wall Street Journal Europe*.

Nickell, S. (1997) 'Unemployment and Labour Market Rigidities: Europe versus North America', *Journal of Economic Perspectives*, Vol. 11, No. 3.

OECD (1994) *Country report on France*, Paris.

OECD (1995) *Country report on France*, Paris.

OECD (1997) *Country report on France*, Paris.

OECD (1998) *OECD Economic Outlook*.

Oppenheimer, P. and Forder J. (1996) 'The Changing Rationale of Monetary Union' in Hayward, J. (ed) *Elitism, Populism and European Politics*, OUP, Oxford.

Pennant-Rea, R. *et al.* (1997) *The Ostrich and the EMU: policy choices facing the United Kingdom*, Centre for Economic Policy Research, London.

Porter, R.D. and Judson, R.A. (1996, October) 'The location of US currency: how much of it is abroad?', *Federal Reserve Bulletin*, Vol. 82.

Ramaswamy, R. and Sloek, T. (1997, December) 'The real effects of monetary policy in the European Union: what are the differences?', International Monetary Fund Working Paper WP/97/160.

Redwood, J. (1997) *Our currency, our country: the dangers of European Monetary Union*, London.

Sachs, J. and Sala-I-Martin, X. (1992) 'Fiscal Federalism and Optimum currency areas: evidence from Europe and the United States', in Canzoneri, M., Grilli, V. and Masson, P. (eds) *Establishing a Central Bank: issues in Europe and lessons from the US*.

Samuelson, P. (1964, May) 'Theoretical notes on trade problems', *Review of Economics and Statistics*.

Szymanski, S. (1994, September) 'The City Labour market', in *The City Research Project*, Corporation of London.

Thygesen, N. (1998, May) 'EMU, Britain and other outsiders', Special Paper No. 102, Financial Markets Group, London School of Economics.

Vinals, J. and Jimeno, J.F. 'Monetary Union and European Unemployment', Documento de Trabajo No. 9624, Servicio de Estudios, Banco de Espana.

Von Hagen, J. (1992) 'Fiscal Arrangements in a monetary union: evidence from the US', in Fair, S. and de Boissieu, C. (eds) *Fiscal Policy, Taxes and the Financial System in an Increasingly Integrated Europe*, Kluwer, Dordrecht.

Index